BASICS OF KEYBOARD THEORY

LEVEL 10
(ADVANCED LEVEL)

Third Edition

Julie McIntosh Johnson

J. Johnson Music Publications
P.O. Box 230
Lockwood, CA 93932
Phone: (714) 961-0257
Fax: (714) 242-9350
www.bktmusic.com
info@bktmusic.com

Basics of Keyboard Theory, Level 10 (Advanced Level)
Third Edition

Published by:

J. Johnson Music Publications
P.O. Box 230
Lockwood, CA 93932 U.S.A.
(714) 961-0257
www.bktmusic.com

Library of Congress Cataloging in Publication Data

Johnson, Julie Anne McIntosh
Basics of Keyboard Theory, Level 10

ISBN 10: 1-891757-38-5
ISBN 13: 978-1891757-38-9

LC TX 4-721-490

TO THE TEACHER

Basics of Keyboard Theory, Level 10 (Advanced Level) includes brief reviews of basic theory elements and detailed analysis of music literature. The user should be an advanced music student with a strong understanding of theory (keys, chord analysis, figured bass, etc.). It is highly recommended that the student complete *Basics of Keyboard Theory, Level 9* before attempting this book.

This workbook corresponds with the Music Teachers' Association of California Certificate of Merit® Piano Syllabus. In addition to covering those requirements, several other theory elements are included. These are to help prepare students for college theory courses. A student who completes Levels 9 and 10 of this series will have a very good foundation in music theory.

The theory concepts in *Basics of Keyboard Theory, Level 10* may be applied to music that the student is currently performing in order to enhance the interpretation and performance of the music.

Ear Training Basics
Levels Preparatory through 10

by
Julie Johnson
Author of *Basics of Keyboard Theory*

Ear
Training
Basics

Julie McIntosh Johnson

J. Johnson Music Publications

- An innovative teaching approach helps minimize student guessing.
- Separate student and teacher books provide the framework for a collaborative learning experience.
- Teacher Books include activities to be completed at the lesson, teaching tips, and answers for the student home assignments.
- Student Books include worksheets and an MP3 CD.

www.bktmusic.com

J. Johnson Music Publications
info@bktmusic.com

Julie Johnson's Guide to
AP* Music Theory, Second Edition

Julie Johnson's
Guide to

AP*
Music
Theory

Second Edition, with Downloadable Audio

Julie McIntosh Johnson

J. Johnson Music Publications

* AP and Advanced Placement are trademarks registered and/or owned by the College Board, which was not involved in the production of, and does not endorse, this product.

- Follows requirements of the College Board Advanced Placement* Music Theory exam
- Edited and expanded based on customer feedback
- More progressive sight-singing and ear-training
- New In-Class ear-training pages for instructor and student collaboration
- More "free response" assignments
- Practice test and grading guidelines
- Supplementary materials available online
- Downloadable audio files at www.juliejohnsontheory.com

*AP and Advanced Placement are trademarks registered and/or owned by the College Board, which was not involved in the production of, and does not endorse, this product.

TABLE OF CONTENTS

Basics of Keyboard Theory, Advanced Level is dedicated to my husband Rob, who fixed my computer more than once, my children Robert and Jeff, who often had to wait patiently for me to finish just "one more section," and to the Lord, Who gave me the strength and ability to complete the book.

LESSON 1: KEYS, SCALES AND INTERVALS

Key signatures are found at the beginning of a composition. The key signature indicates the key or tonality of the music, and which notes will receive sharps or flats. Sharps are in this order: F C G D A E B. Flats are in this order: B E A D G C F.

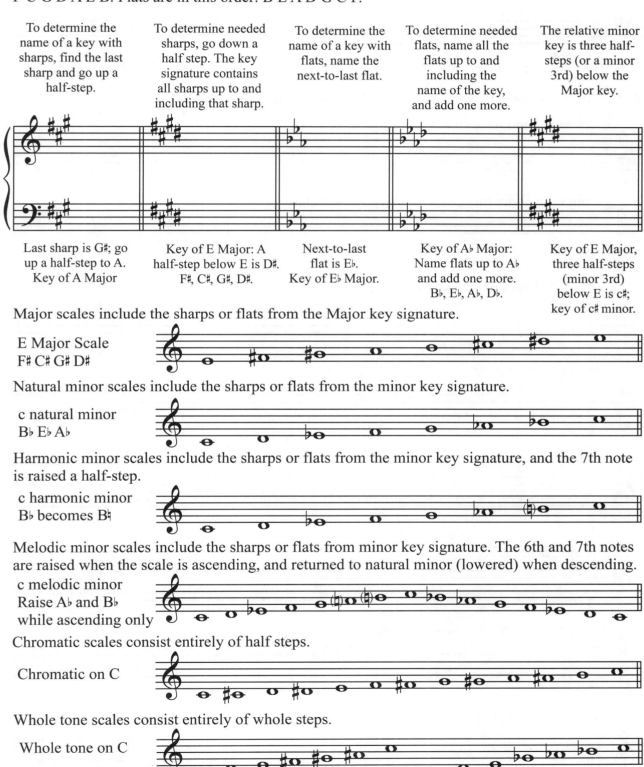

To determine the name of a key with sharps, find the last sharp and go up a half-step.

To determine needed sharps, go down a half step. The key signature contains all sharps up to and including that sharp.

To determine the name of a key with flats, name the next-to-last flat.

To determine needed flats, name all the flats up to and including the name of the key, and add one more.

The relative minor key is three half-steps (or a minor 3rd) below the Major key.

Last sharp is G♯; go up a half-step to A. Key of A Major

Key of E Major: A half-step below E is D♯. F♯, C♯, G♯, D♯.

Next-to-last flat is E♭. Key of E♭ Major.

Key of A♭ Major: Name flats up to A♭ and add one more. B♭, E♭, A♭, D♭.

Key of E Major, three half-steps (minor 3rd) below E is c♯; key of c♯ minor.

Major scales include the sharps or flats from the Major key signature.

E Major Scale
F♯ C♯ G♯ D♯

Natural minor scales include the sharps or flats from the minor key signature.

c natural minor
B♭ E♭ A♭

Harmonic minor scales include the sharps or flats from the minor key signature, and the 7th note is raised a half-step.

c harmonic minor
B♭ becomes B♮

Melodic minor scales include the sharps or flats from minor key signature. The 6th and 7th notes are raised when the scale is ascending, and returned to natural minor (lowered) when descending.

c melodic minor
Raise A♭ and B♭
while ascending only

Chromatic scales consist entirely of half steps.

Chromatic on C

Whole tone scales consist entirely of whole steps.

Whole tone on C

or

2

1. Notate each of the following key signatures in both clefs.

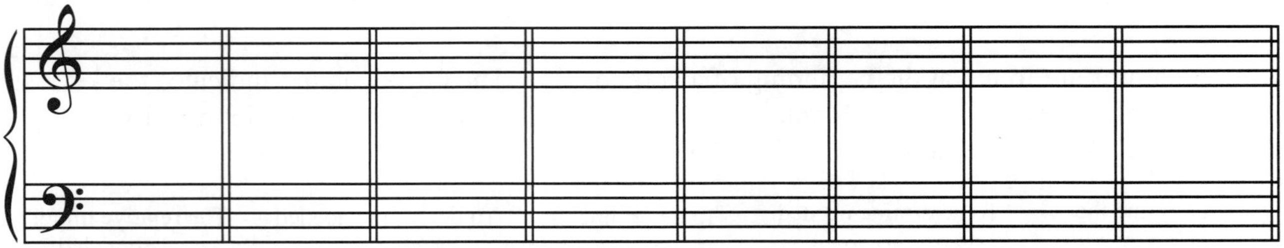

B Major   b♭ minor   C♯ Major   G♭ Major   a♭ minor   f minor   D Major   E♭ Major

2. Notate each of the following scales using accidentals (not key signatures).

Chromatic beginning on F, ascending

g♯ minor, melodic form, ascending and descending

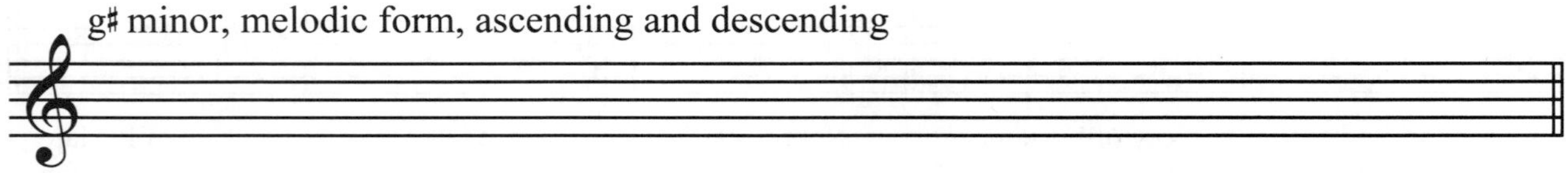

Chromatic beginning on G, descending

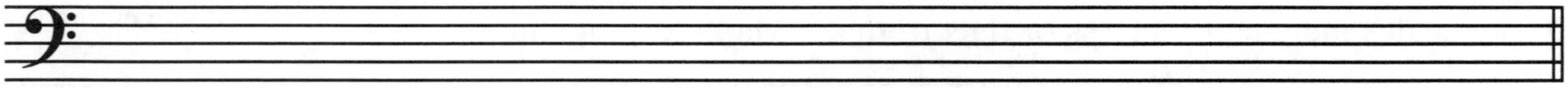

b minor, harmonic form, descending

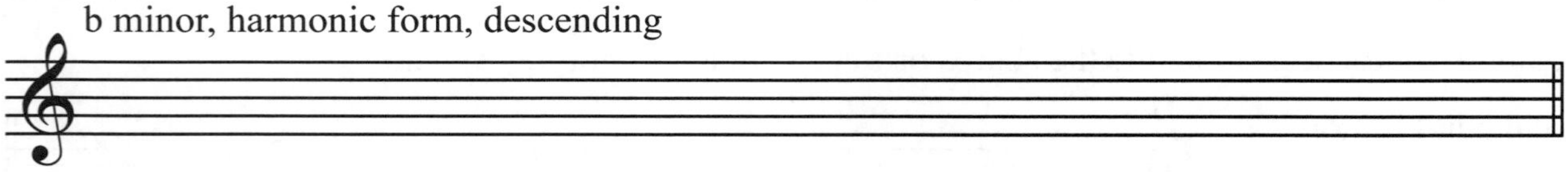

F♯ Major, ascending

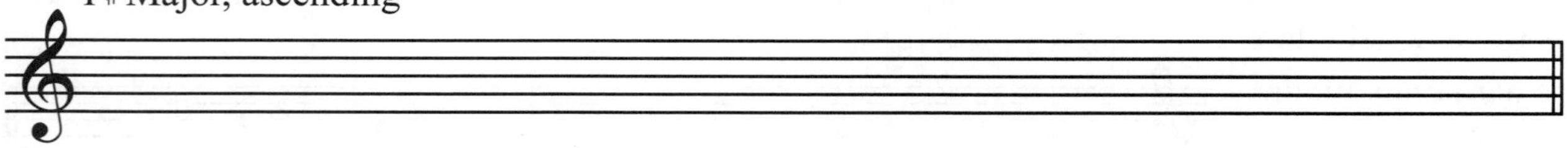

B Major, descending

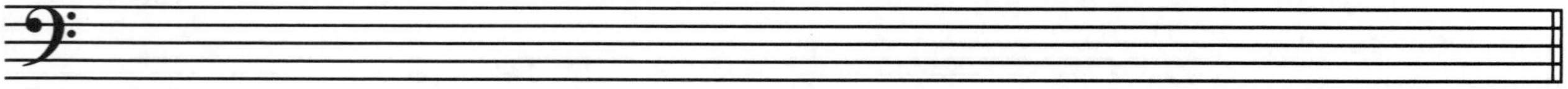

Whole tone beginning on A, ascending

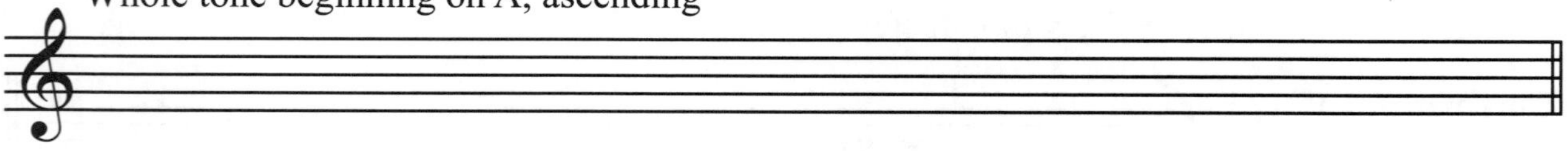

A♭ Major, descending

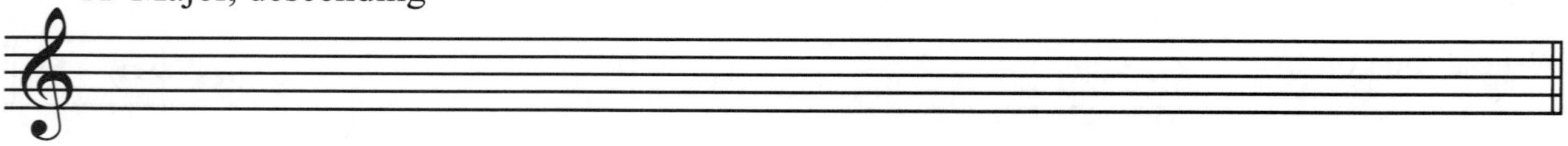

An **Interval** is the distance between two notes. Intervals are named with qualities and numbers. To find the number, count the two notes that form the interval and all the notes between the two. Qualities are Major (M), minor (m), diminished (d) or Augmented (A). To find the quality, use the Major key signature of the lowest note and the following directions.

Both notes are in the key	M2 M3 M6 M7 P4 P5 P8
Top note is lowered a half step	m2 m3 m6 m7 d4 d5 d8
Top note is lowered a whole step	d2 d3 d6 d7
Top note is raised a half step	Augmented (all intervals)

3. Name each of the following intervals.

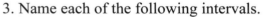

_____   _____   _____   _____   _____   _____   _____   _____

4. Draw a note above each given note to complete the following intervals.

M6   m7   A4   M2   d4   A2   P5   m3

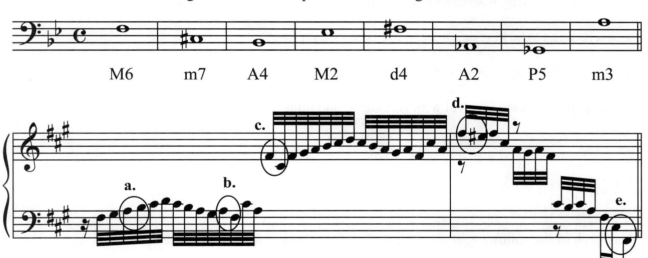

Answer the following questions about the music above.   J.S. Bach: *Toccata, BWV 910*

5. What is the key? _____ _____

6. The entire example is made of which scale? _____ _____

7. Name each circled interval with its number and quality.   a. _____

b. _____

c. _____

d. _____

e. _____

Beethoven: *Sonata, Op. 81a*

Answer the following questions about music above.

8. According to the key signature, what is the Major key? _____ _____

9. The first three measures of the treble clef are made up of which scale? _____ _____

10. Name each circled interval with its quality and number.   a. _____

                                                          b. _____

                                                           c. _____

                                                           d. _____

                                                           e. _____

Mark each of the following statements with T for true or F for false.

11. _____ To determine the relative minor of a Major key, go up three half steps.

12. _____ If the top note of a Major interval is lowered a half-step, the interval becomes minor.

13. _____ If the top note of Perfect interval is raised a half-step, the interval becomes Augmented.

14. _____ To determine the name of a key with flats, name the last flat.

15. _____ To determine the name of a key with sharps, go up a whole step above the last sharp.

16. _____ If the top note of a Major interval is lowered a whole-step, the interval becomes diminished.

LESSON 2: MODES

The term **MODE** is used to indicate any of a number of scale formations, including Major and minor. Most commonly, the term is associated with the following scale patterns.

IONIAN MODE is the same as the Major scale. Half-steps are between notes 3-4 and 7-8.

IONIAN MODE ON C (C MAJOR SCALE)

DORIAN MODE: Begins and ends on the **SECOND** note of the Major scale.
  Half-steps are between notes 2-3 and 6-7.
  The Major scale becomes Dorian mode by lowering the 3rd and 7th scale degrees a half-step.

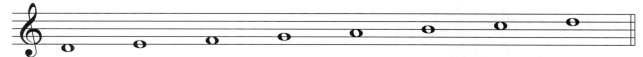

DORIAN MODE ON D

PHRYGIAN MODE: Begins and ends on the **THIRD** note of the Major scale.
  Half-steps are between notes 1-2 and 5-6.
  The Major scale becomes Phrygian mode by lowering scale degrees 2, 3, 6, and 7 a half-step.

PHRYGIAN MODE ON E

LYDIAN MODE: Begins and ends on the **FOURTH** note of the Major scale.
  Half-steps are between notes 4-5 and 7-8.
  The Major scale becomes Lydian by raising the 4th scale degree a half-step.

LYDIAN MODE ON F

MIXOLYDIAN MODE: Begins and ends on the **FIFTH** note of the Major scale.
  Half-steps are between notes 3-4 and 6-7.
  The Major scale becomes Mixolydian by lowering the 7th scale degree a half-step.

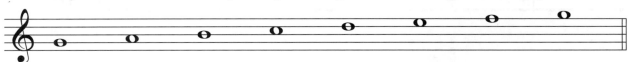

MIXOLYDIAN MODE ON G

AEOLIAN MODE: Begins and ends on the **SIXTH** note of the Major scale.
  It is the same as natural minor.
  Half-steps occur between notes 2-3 and 5-6.
  The Major scale becomes Aeolian mode by lowering scale degrees 3, 6, and 7 a half-step.

AEOLIAN MODE ON A (A NATURAL MINOR SCALE)

LOCRIAN MODE: Begins and ends on the **SEVENTH** note of the Major scale.
  Half-steps occur between notes 1-2 and 4-5.
  The Major scale becomes Locrian mode by lowering scale degrees 2, 3, 5, 6, and 7 a half-step.

LOCRIAN MODE ON B

NAMING MODES

1. Look at the accidentals and determine the Major key signature that uses them.
2. Count up from the name of that Major key to the starting note of the mode.
3. Match the name of the mode with the associated scale degree.

1. Sharps are F♯ and C♯; D Major key signature
2. A is the fifth note of D Major
3. Mixoydian Mode

Name of Mode	Major Scale Degree:	Interval to Descend to Find Key Signature	Locations of Half-Steps		Scale Degree Changes
Ionian	1	None	3-4	7-8	None
Dorian	2	M2	2-3	6-7	3 and 7 Lowered
Phrygian	3	M3	1-2	5-6	2, 3, 6, and 7 Lowered
Lydian	4	P4	4-5	7-8	4 Raised
Mixolydian	5	P5	3-4	6-7	7 Lowered
Aeolian	6	M6	2-3	5-6	3, 6, and 7 Lowered
Locrian	7	M7	1-2	4-5	2, 3, 5, 6, & 7 Lowered

Fill in the blanks for each example to determine the name of the mode. The first one is given.

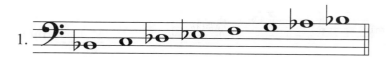

1.

a. Accidentals are: __B♭__, __D♭__, __E♭__, __A♭__

b. Key signature order:
   __B♭__, __E♭__, __A♭__, __D♭__

c. Name of Major key: __A♭__

d. Count up from name of key to first note of mode: __A♭ to B♭: 2nd note__

e. Name of mode: __Dorian__

2.

a. Accidentals are: ___, ___, ___, ___

b. Key signature order:

   ___, ___, ___, ___

c. Name of Major key: _____

d. Count up from name of key to first note of mode: _____

e. Name of mode: _____

3.

a. Accidental is: _____

b. Key signature order: _____

c. Name of Major key: _____

d. Count up from name of key to first note of mode: _____

e. Name of mode: _____

4.

a. Accidentals are: _____, _____

b. Key signature order: _____, _____

c. Name of Major key: _____

d. Count up from name of key to first note of mode: _____

e. Name of mode: _____

8

5. Name each of the following modes.

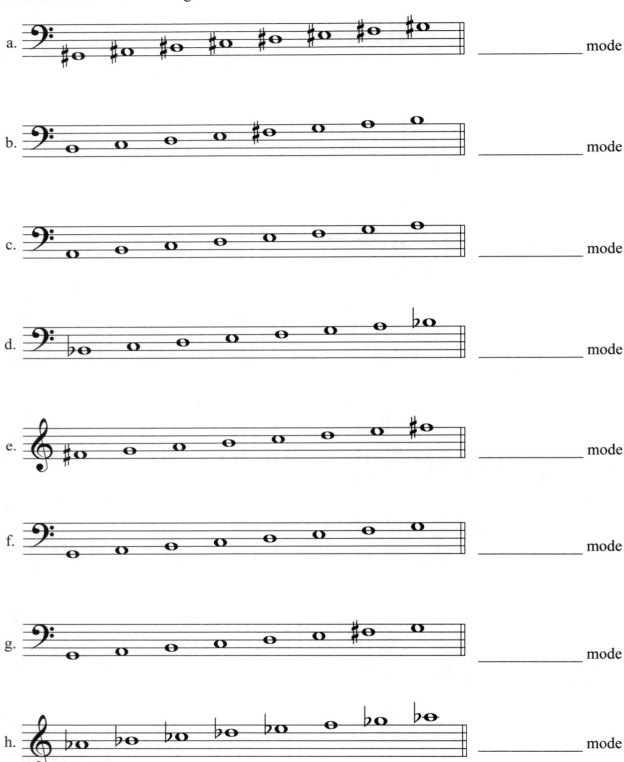

a. _____ mode

b. _____ mode

c. _____ mode

d. _____ mode

e. _____ mode

f. _____ mode

g. _____ mode

h. _____ mode

Certificate of Merit® requirements: Modes with no sharps or flats,
with one sharp (F♯) and with one flat (B♭)

THREE WAYS TO DETERMINE WHICH SHARPS OR FLATS ARE IN A MODE

METHOD 1

1. Starting with the letter name of the mode, go down the interval listed on the chart below.

2. Use the key signature for that note.

PHRYGIAN MODE ON G

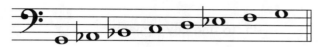

1. Go down a M3 below G
2. Use E♭ Major Key Signature

METHOD 2

1. Draw the notes without any sharps or flats.

2. Add accidentals where needed to form the correct location of half-steps and whole-steps.

MIXOLYDIAN MODE ON A

1. Draw A to A with no accidentals

half-step   half-step

2. Add accidentals to form half-steps between notes 3-4 and 6-7.

METHOD 3

1. Notate the Major scale beginning on the required note.

2. Change the scale degrees using the chart below.

DORIAN MODE ON B

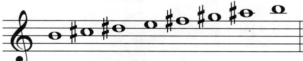

1. Notate B Major Scale

2. Lower scale degrees 3 and 7

Name of Mode	Major Scale Degree:	Interval to Descend to Find Key Signature	Locations of Half-Steps		Scale Degree Changes
Ionian	1	None	3-4	7-8	None
Dorian	2	M2	2-3	6-7	3 and 7 Lowered
Phrygian	3	M3	1-2	5-6	2, 3, 6, and 7 Lowered
Lydian	4	P4	4-5	7-8	4 Raised
Mixolydian	5	P5	3-4	6-7	7 Lowered
Aeolian	6	M6	2-3	5-6	3, 6, and 7 Lowered
Locrian	7	M7	1-2	4-5	2, 3, 5, 6, & 7 Lowered

10

Fill in the blanks for each example, then add the accidentals to complete each mode. The first one is given.

6. a. Go down the interval of a

   _P5_ to find key signature

   b. Major key: __F__

   c. Key signature: ___B♭___

   Mixolydian Mode on C

7. a. Go down the interval of a

   ____ to find key signature

   b. Major key: ____

   c. Key signature: _____

   Ionian Mode on F♯

8. a. Go down the interval of a

   ____ to find key signature

   b. Major key: ____

   c. Key signature: _____

   Phrygian Mode on E

9. a. Go down the interval of a

   ____ to find key signature

   b. Major key: ____

   c. Key signature: _____

   Lydian Mode on A♭

10. a. Go down the interval of a

    ____ to find key signature

    b. Major key: ____

    c. Key signature: _____

    Locrian Mode on B♭

11. Notate each of the following modes.

a.

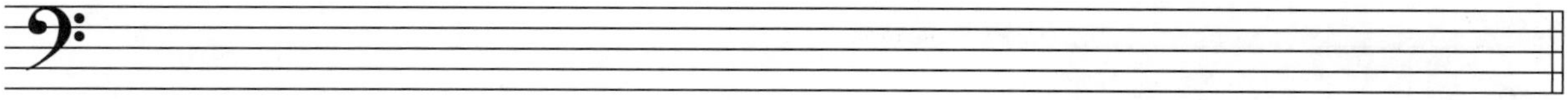

Dorian Mode on G

b.

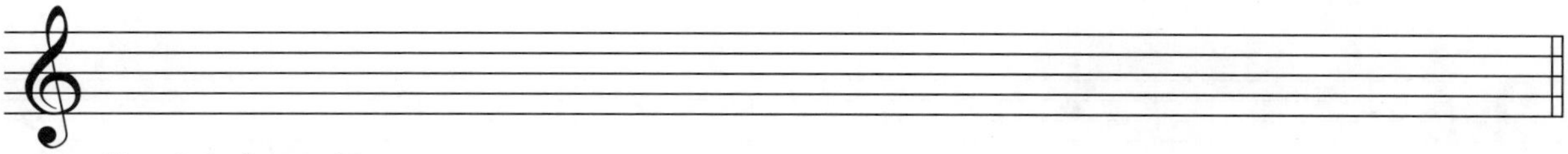

Aeolian Mode on D

c.

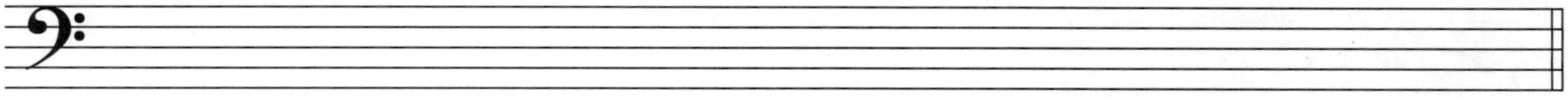

Phrygian Mode on A

d.

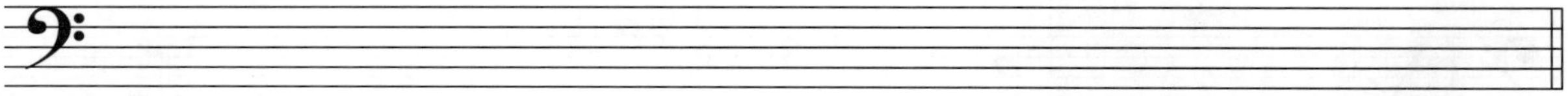

Mixolydian Mode on D

e.

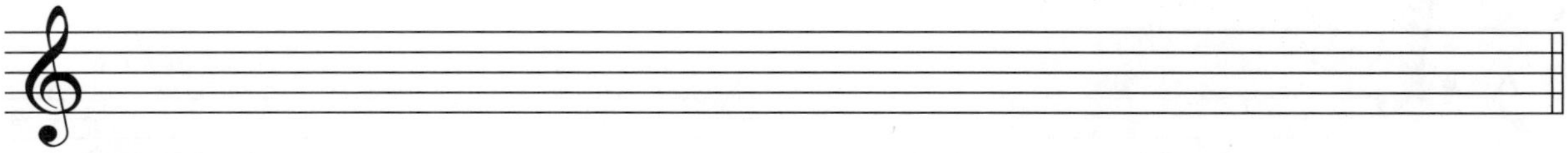

Ionian Mode on G

f.

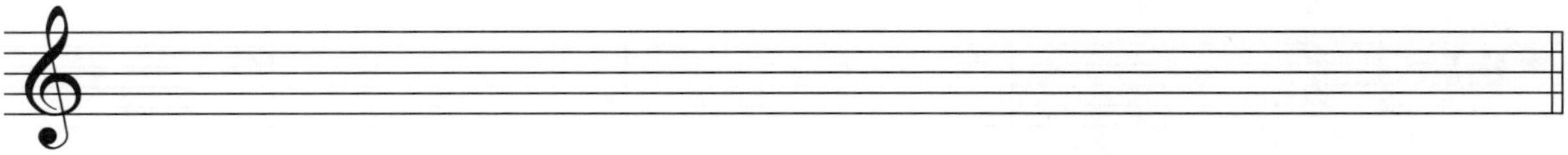

Locrian Mode on F♯

g.

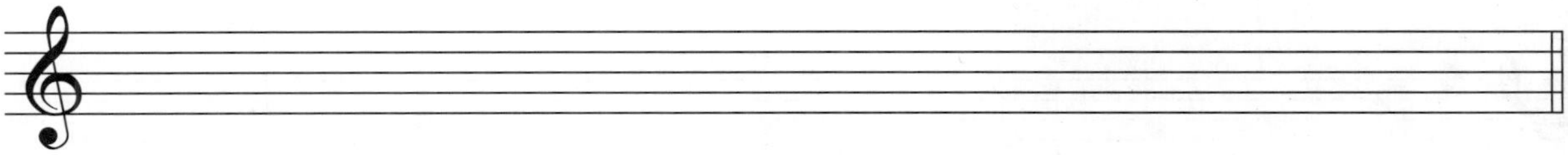

Lydian Mode on C

h.

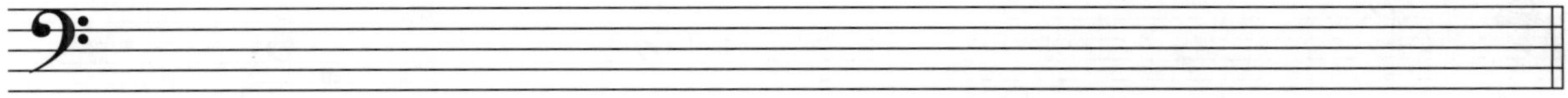

Aeolian Mode on E

12. Each of the following examples is modal. Name each mode.

a. _____ mode

b. _____ mode

c. _____ mode

LESSON 3: CHORDS

Triads are chords that contain three notes and are based on the interval of a third.

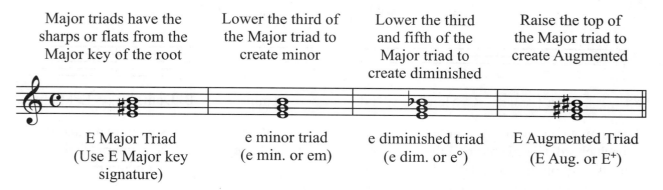

Major triads have the sharps or flats from the Major key of the root	Lower the third of the Major triad to create minor	Lower the third and fifth of the Major triad to create diminished	Raise the top of the Major triad to create Augmented
E Major Triad (Use E Major key signature)	e minor triad (e min. or em)	e diminished triad (e dim. or e°)	E Augmented Triad (E Aug. or E⁺)

Seventh chords have four notes. The fourth note is a 7th above the root.

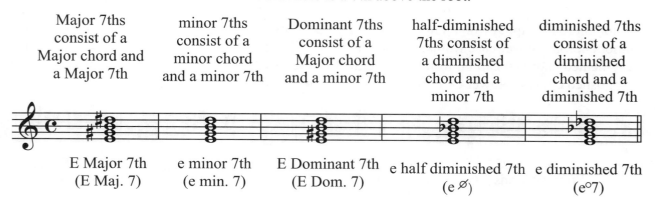

Major 7ths consist of a Major chord and a Major 7th	minor 7ths consist of a minor chord and a minor 7th	Dominant 7ths consist of a Major chord and a minor 7th	half-diminished 7ths consist of a diminished chord and a minor 7th	diminished 7ths consist of a diminished chord and a diminished 7th
E Major 7th (E Maj. 7)	e minor 7th (e min. 7)	E Dominant 7th (E Dom. 7)	e half diminished 7th (e ∅)	e diminished 7th (e°7)

Inversions are created when a note other than the root is lowest. Figured bass is used to identify inversions. Figured bass is determined by the intervals present above the lowest note.

Inversions of triads: Inversions of 7th chords:

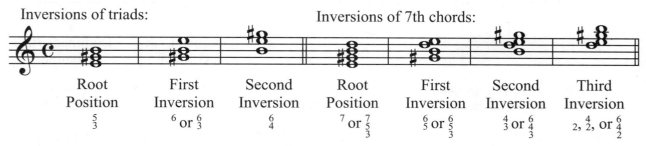

Root Position $\frac{5}{3}$	First Inversion 6 or $\frac{6}{3}$	Second Inversion $\frac{6}{4}$	Root Position 7 or $\frac{7}{5}{}_{3}$	First Inversion $\frac{6}{5}$ or $\frac{6}{5}{}_{3}$	Second Inversion $\frac{4}{3}$ or $\frac{6}{4}{}_{3}$	Third Inversion 2, $\frac{4}{2}$, or $\frac{6}{4}{}_{2}$

1. Name each of the following chords with its root, quality and figured bass.

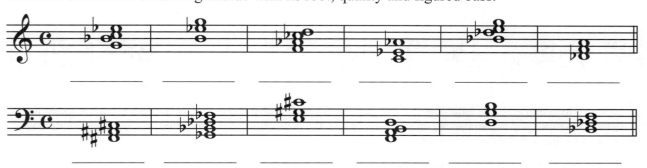

2. Using whole notes, notate each of the following chords.

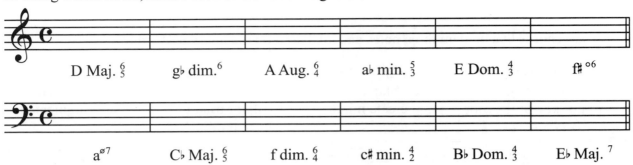

Triads may be built on each note of the scale. Sharps or flats from the key signature are included in each chord. Chords built on the first, fourth and fifth scale degrees are the primary triads. Chords built on the second, third, sixth and seventh scale degrees are the secondary triads. When writing the primary and secondary triads in minor keys, harmonic minor is typically used. The key signature will determine the quality of each chord.

Major chords = capital Roman numerals: I IV V VI [1]
minor chords = lower case Roman numerals: i   ii   iii   iv   vi
Augmented chords = capital Roman numerals followed by $^+$: III$^+$
diminished chords = lower case Roman numerals followed by °: ii°   vii°

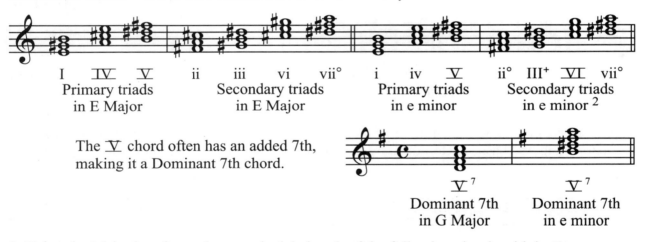

The V chord often has an added 7th, making it a Dominant 7th chord.

3. Using the Major key for each example, label each of the following chords with its Roman numeral and figured bass. For Major chords, draw lines above and below the Roman numerals.

[1] When Roman numerals are hand-written, lines are often drawn above and below the Roman numerals for capital letters. When Roman numerals are computer-generated, the distinction between capital and lower-case letters is obvious so the lines are not necessary.

[2] In compositions, III+ is rare. III is usually Major.

4. Using the minor key for each example, notate each of the following chords.

ii°   iv⁶   VI   i⁶₄   V⁷   VI⁶₃

vii°   V   V⁴₂   VI⁶₄   ii°   iv⁶₄

Beethoven: *Sonata, Op. 81a*

Answer the following questions about the music above.

5. According to the key signature, what is the Major key? 	_____ _____

6. Name chords **a** through **e** with their roots, qualities, and figured bass.

a. _____

b. _____

c. _____

d. _____

e. _____

7. Name chords **f** through **h** with their Roman numerals and figured bass.

f. _____

g. _____

h. _____

Chopin: *Mazurka, Op. 50, No. 2*

Answer the following questions about the above example.

8. What is the key?

     _____ _____

9. Name each circled chord with its Roman numeral and figured bass.

     a. _____

     b. _____

     c. _____

     d. _____

     e. _____

10. Name each boxed chord with its root, quality and figured bass.

     1. _____

     2. _____

     3. _____

LESSON 4: THE SECONDARY DOMINANT

Frequently, chords appear that are not within the key of the composition. One of these is the **SECONDARY DOMINANT**. Secondary dominants add color and variety to the music.

The secondary dominant is the Dominant ($\underline{V}$) or Dominant seventh ($\underline{V}^7$) of a key other than tonic (I). It typically resolves to the chord that is tonic of the key to which it belongs.

Secondary dominants include accidentals that are not in the key signature, and their qualities are different from those of the primary and secondary triads.

Examples in the key of C Major:

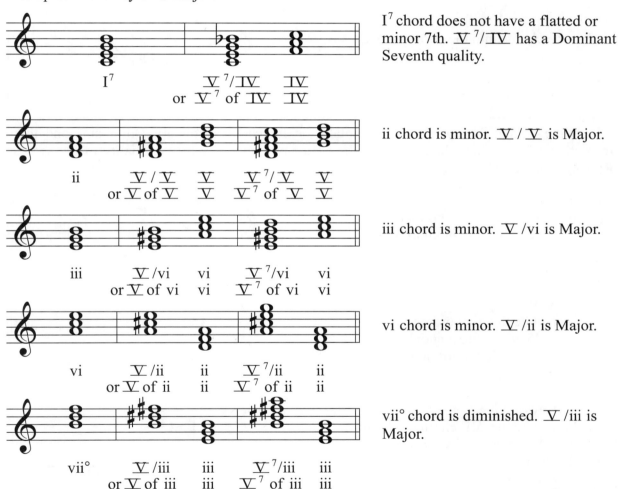

$I^7 \qquad \underline{V}^7/\underline{IV} \qquad \underline{IV}$
or $\underline{V}^7$ of $\underline{IV}$ $\underline{IV}$

I^7 chord does not have a flatted or minor 7th. $\underline{V}^7/\underline{IV}$ has a Dominant Seventh quality.

ii $\qquad \underline{V}/\underline{V} \qquad \underline{V} \qquad \underline{V}^7/\underline{V} \qquad \underline{V}$
or $\underline{V}$ of $\underline{V}$ $\underline{V}$ $\underline{V}^7$ of $\underline{V}$ $\underline{V}$

ii chord is minor. $\underline{V}/\underline{V}$ is Major.

iii $\qquad \underline{V}/vi \qquad vi \qquad \underline{V}^7/vi \qquad vi$
or $\underline{V}$ of vi $\quad$ vi $\quad \underline{V}^7$ of vi $\quad$ vi

iii chord is minor. $\underline{V}/vi$ is Major.

vi $\qquad \underline{V}/ii \qquad ii \qquad \underline{V}^7/ii \qquad ii$
or $\underline{V}$ of ii $\quad$ ii $\quad \underline{V}^7$ of ii $\quad$ ii

vi chord is minor. $\underline{V}/ii$ is Major.

vii° $\qquad \underline{V}/iii \qquad iii \qquad \underline{V}^7/iii \qquad iii$
or $\underline{V}$ of iii $\quad$ iii $\quad \underline{V}^7$ of iii $\quad$ iii

vii° chord is diminished. $\underline{V}/iii$ is Major.

The **SECONDARY LEADING TONE** chord is the vii° or vii°^{7} of a key other than tonic.

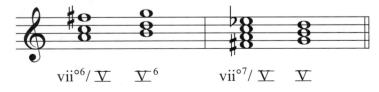

vii°^{6}/$\underline{V}$ $\quad \underline{V}^6 \qquad$ vii°^{7}/$\underline{V}$ $\quad \underline{V}$

18

To notate secondary dominants and their resolutions:

1. Find and notate the <u>second</u> chord (the resolution).

$\underline{V}\,{}^6_5/$ iii   iii

2. Find the $\underline{V}$ or $\underline{V}^7$ chord of the resolution.

The root of the Secondary Dominant and the fifth of the resolution will be the same note. Notate the Major or Dominant 7th chord in root position.

$\underline{V}\,{}^7/$iii   iii

3. Put the chords into the correct positions.

$\underline{V}\,{}^6_5/$iii   iii
or $\underline{V}\,{}^6_5/$iii   iii

1. Fill in the blanks. Using half notes, notate the indicated Secondary Dominants and their resolutions. Determine whether to use the Major or minor key by the quality of the second Roman Numeral. Use the harmonic form for minor keys.

    a. Key of _____ _____.
    b. Notate the iii$^6_4$ chord on the staff.
    c. A P5 above the iii chord is _____.
    d. Notate a $\underline{V}^7$ chord on the root named in
        question c.

$\underline{V}\,{}^7/$iii   iii$^6_4$

    a. Key of _____ _____.
    b. Notate the ii$^6_4$ chord on the staff.
    c. A P5 above the ii chord is _____.
    d. Notate a $\underline{V}$ chord on the root named in
        question c.

$\underline{V}\,/$ii   ii$^6_4$

    a. Key of _____ _____.
    b. Notate the $\underline{VI}$ chord on the staff.
    c. A P5 above the $\underline{VI}$ chord is _____.
    d. Notate a $\underline{V}\,{}^6_5$ chord on the root named in
        question c.

$\underline{V}\,{}^6_5/\underline{VI}$ $\underline{VI}$

    a. Key of _____ _____.
    b. Notate the iv chord on the staff.
    c. A P5 above the iv chord is _____.
    d. Notate a $\underline{V}\,{}^6_5$ chord on the root named in
        question c.

$\underline{V}\,{}^6_5/$iv   iv

2. Using half notes, notate the following Secondary Dominants and their resolutions.

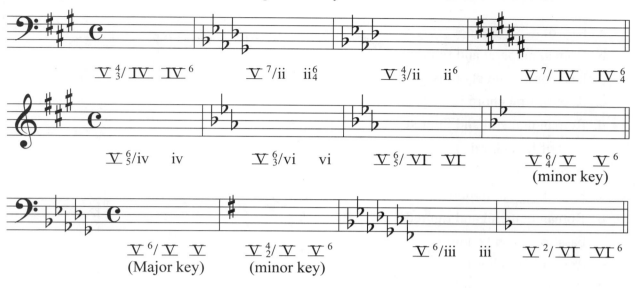

$\underline{V}^{4}_{3}/\underline{IV}$ $\underline{IV}^{6}$ $\underline{V}^{7}/ii$ ii^{6}_{4} $\underline{V}^{4}_{3}/ii$ ii^{6} $\underline{V}^{7}/\underline{IV}$ $\underline{IV}^{6}_{4}$

$\underline{V}^{6}_{5}/iv$ iv $\underline{V}^{6}_{3}/vi$ vi $\underline{V}^{6}_{5}/\underline{VI}$ $\underline{VI}$ $\underline{V}^{6}_{4}/\underline{V}$ $\underline{V}^{6}$
(minor key)

$\underline{V}^{6}/\underline{V}$ $\underline{V}$ $\underline{V}^{4}_{2}/\underline{V}$ $\underline{V}^{6}$ $\underline{V}^{6}/iii$ iii $\underline{V}^{2}/\underline{VI}$ $\underline{VI}^{6}$
(Major key)   (minor key)

To label Secondary Dominants:

1. Determine the key.

2. Label the second chord (the resolution) with its Roman numeral and figured bass.

D♭ Major: ___ / ___   vi

3. The Roman numeral for the second half of the Secondary Dominant will be the same as the resolution. Write the Roman numeral for the resolution after the /. Do not include the figured bass.

D♭ Major: ___ / vi   vi

4. The first half of the Secondary Dominant will be a Dominant or Dominant Seventh chord. Label the first chord with $\underline{V}$ and the appropriate figured figured bass.

D♭ Major: $\underline{V}^{4}_{3}/vi$ vi

Fill in the blanks. Label each chord with its Roman numeral and figured bass.

3. a. Key of _____ minor
   b. Roman numeral and figured
      bass for second chord is _____
   c. Root of first chord is _____
   d. Roman numeral and figured
      bass of first chord is _____ / _____

      _____ / _____   _____

4. a. Key of _____ minor
   b. Roman numeral and figured
      bass for second chord is _____
   c. Root of first chord is _____
   d. Roman numeral and figured
      bass of first chord is _____ / _____

      _____ / _____   _____

5. a. Key of _____ Major
   b. Roman numeral and figured
      bass for second chord is _____
   c. Root of first chord is _____
   d. Roman numeral and figured
      bass of first chord is _____ / _____

      _____ / _____   _____

6. a. Key of _____ Major
   b. Roman numeral and figured
      bass for second chord is _____
   c. Root of first chord is _____
   d. Roman numeral and figured
      bass of first chord is _____ / _____

      _____ / _____   _____

7. a. Key of _____ Major
   b. Roman numeral and figured
      bass for second chord is _____
   c. Root of first chord is _____
   d. Roman numeral and figured
      bass of first chord is _____ / _____

      _____ / _____   _____

8. For each of the following examples, label the boxed chords with Roman numerals and figured bass.

a. From *Sonata, Op. 81a* by Beethoven.

Key of _____ Major: ____ / ____   ____   ____ / ____   ____

b. From *Toccata, BWV 914,* by J.S. Bach.

____ / ____   ____

Key of _____ minor

c. From *Mazurka, Op. 68, No. 1*, by Chopin.

Key of _____ Major: ____ / ____ ____

d. From *Sonata, Op. 90*, by Beethoven.

Key of _____ Major: ____ / ____ ____

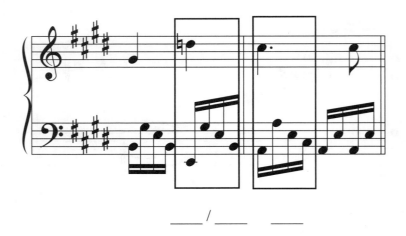

____ / ____ ____

LESSON 5: CADENCES, CHORD PROGRESSIONS, AUGMENTED SIXTH CHORDS

Cadences occur at the ends of phrases or sections in a composition. They act as resting points for the music.

Authentic Cadence: $\underline{V}$ or $\underline{V}^7$ followed by I. Authentic cadences have a stable sound.

AUTHENTIC CADENCES

Plagal Cadence: $\underline{IV}$ followed by I. They sound stable and appear most often in minor keys.

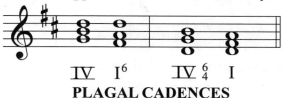

PLAGAL CADENCES

Half Cadence: ends on $\underline{V}$ or $\underline{V}^7$. They sound unstable and typically occur when the music is continuing.

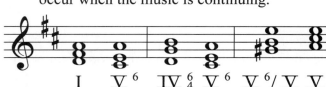

HALF CADENCES

Deceptive Cadence: $\underline{V}$ (or $\underline{IV}$) followed by vi. They sound unstable and typically occur when the music is continuing.

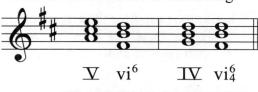

DECEPTIVE CADENCES

A **CHORD PROGRESSION** or **MIXED CADENCE** contains a combination of chords. A smooth progression is created by using **common tones**, notes that remain the same when the chord changes. The following chord progression **MODULATES** to a new key.

A **PIVOT CHORD** is a chord that precedes a key change, and is common to both the original key and the key to which the music modulates. The pivot chord is circled in this example.

Modulation
F Major to C Major

Pivot chord: Acts as I in F Major and $\underline{IV}$ in C Major

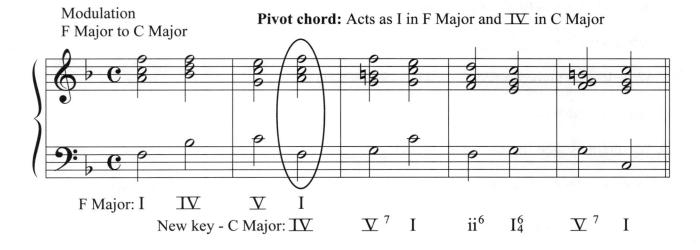

24

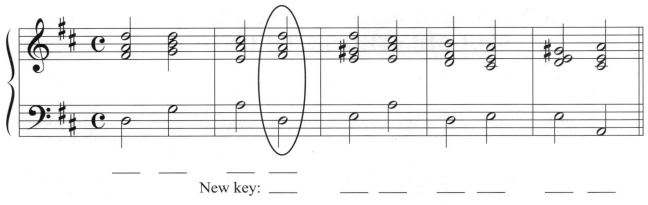

_____ _____   _____ _____

New key: _____   _____ _____   _____ _____   _____ _____

Answer questions 1-5 about the above progression.

1. Write Roman numerals and figured bass for the first four chords.

2. To what key does the example modulate? _____ _____

3. Using the new key, write the Roman numerals and figured bass for the last seven chords.

4. What term is used for the circled chord? _____

5. With what type of cadence does the example end? (Write the name, not the Roman numerals.)

_____

_____ _____   _____ _____   _____ _____   _____ _____

Answer questions 6-10 about the above progression.

6. What is the key? _____ _____

7. Write Roman numerals and figured bass for each chord.

8. Does this example modulate? _____

9. What term is used for the circled chord? _____

10. With what type of cadence does the example end? (Write the name, not the Roman numerals.)

_____

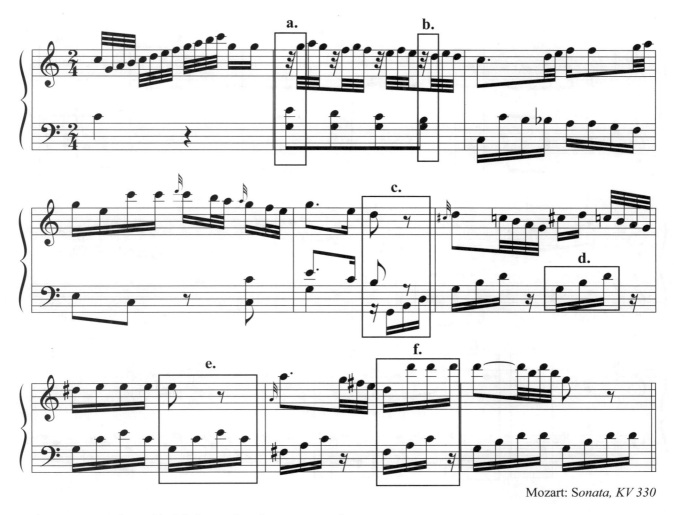

Mozart: *Sonata, KV 330*

Answer questions 11-16 about the above example.

11. What is the key at the beginning of the example? _____ _____

12. To what key does the example modulate? _____ _____

13. Name chords **a**, **b** and **c** with Roman numerals and figured bass, using the key in which the example begins.

   a. _____
   b. _____
   c. _____

14. Using the original key, what type of cadence ends the phrase before the key change (ending with chord **c**)?

   _____

15. Name chords **c**, **d**, **e** and **f** using the new key.

   c. _____
   d. _____
   e. _____
   f. _____

16. Which chord is the pivot chord? (Mark the answer.)

   _____ Chord **c**
   _____ Chord **e**

Haydn: *Sonata, Hob.-Verz. XVI: 27*

Answer questions 17-23 about the above example.

17. What is the key at the beginning of the example?   _____ _____

18. To what key does the music modulate?   _____ _____

19. What is the relationship between the original key
    and the new key? (Mark the answer.)   ___ I-V   ___ I-IV   ___ I-vi

20. Using the original key, name chords **a** through **e**
    with Roman numerals and figured bass.   a. _____ b. _____ c. _____

    d. _____ e. _____

21. Using the new key, name chords **e** through **g**
    with Roman numerals and figured bass.   e. _____ f. _____ g. _____

22. What term is used for chord **c**?   _____

23. What term is used for chord **e**?   _____

Optional, For Extra Study: The Augmented Sixth Chord

The **Augmented 6th chord** is built on the flatted 6th of the key (the flatted submediant), and includes the interval of an Augmented 6th between the root and top notes.

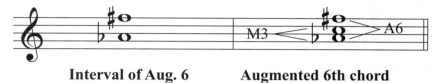

Interval of Aug. 6   **Augmented 6th chord**

There are three types of augmented 6th chords, traditionally called Italian, French, and German. Each includes the augmented 6th plus a Major 3rd above the root. The **Italian Augmented 6th** is formed by those three notes, and normally resolves to the Dominant of the key. A number of different figured bass symbols are acceptable for augmented sixth chords. Italian augmented sixth chords may be identified as follows:

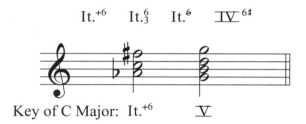

The **French Augmented 6th** includes the three basic notes plus an added Augmented 4th, and usually resolves to the Dominant. The French augmented sixth may be identified as:

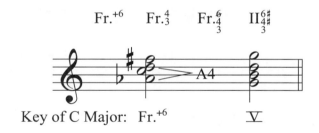

The **German Augmented 6th** includes the three basic notes plus an added Perfect 5th, which may be notated as a doubly Augmented 4th. It may resolve to the Dominant or to Tonic in second inversion. The German augmented sixth may be identified as:

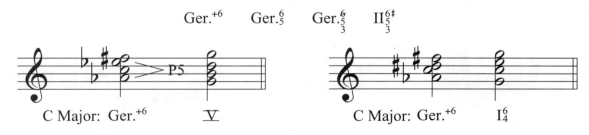

> **The Augmented Sixth chord is not required for the MTAC Certificate of Merit® theory test.**

28

24. Using half notes, notate Italian Augmented 6th chords and their resolutions to Dominant in each of the following Major keys. The first one is given.

It.$^{+6}$ V   It.$^6_3$ V   It.^{6} V   IV $^{6\sharp}$ V

25. Using half notes, notate French Augmented 6th chords and their resolutions to Dominant in each of the following Major keys.

Fr.$^{+6}$ V   Fr.$^4_3$ V   Fr.$^6_{4\atop3}$ V   II$^{6\sharp}_{4\atop3}$ V

26. Using half notes, notate German Augmented 6th chords and the indicated resolutions in the following Major keys.

Ger.$^{+6}$ V   Ger.$^6_5$ V   Ger.$^6_{5\atop3}$ I$^6_4$ II$^{6\sharp}_{5\atop3}$ I$^6_4$

27. Name the key for each of the following examples. Label each boxed Augmented 6th chord. Label each boxed resolution with its Roman numeral and figured bass. The first one is given.

a. From *Sonata, Hob. XVI:48: Andante con expressione* by Haydn.

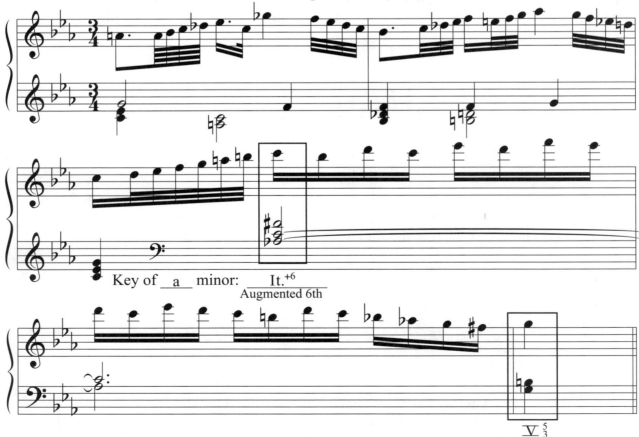

Key of __a__ minor: ___It.$^{+6}$___
Augmented 6th

V $^5_3$

b. From *Sonata, K. 332: Allegro* by Mozart. According to the key signature, this example is in the key of _____ Major. This section of the music is in C Major. **<u>Analyze this excerpt in the key of C Major.</u>**

Key of C Major: _____   _____

c. From *Intermezzo, Op. 117, No. 2* by Brahms. According to the key signature, this example is in the key of _____ minor. **<u>Analyze this excerpt in the key of f minor.</u>**

Key of f minor: _____

_____

d. From *Sonata, K. 332: Allegro* by Mozart.

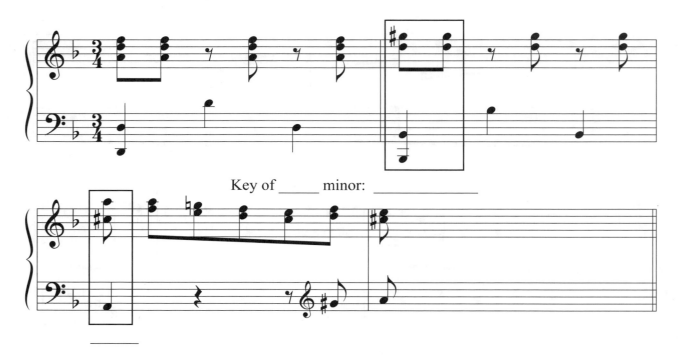

Key of _____ minor: _____

_____

e. From *Ballade, Op. 47* by Chopin.

Key of _____ Major: _____ _____

f. From *Nocturne, Op. 48, No. 2* by Chopin.

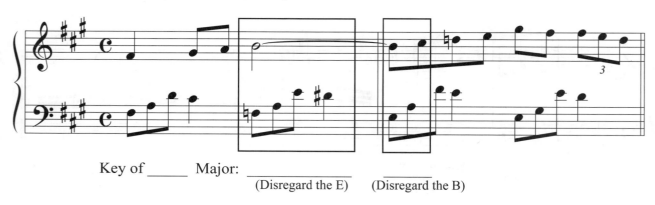

Key of _____ Major: _____ _____
(Disregard the E)   (Disregard the B)

REVIEW: LESSONS 1-5

1. Notate each of the following key signatures in both clefs.

C# Major   bb minor   g# minor   c minor   Db Major   Ab Major

B Major   A Major   g minor   c# minor   F# Major   Cb Major

2. Notate each of the following scales or modes using accidentals, not key signatures.

d minor, melodic form, ascending and descending

Lydian mode beginning on Bb, ascending

f minor, harmonic form, ascending

Whole tone beginning on B, ascending

Chromatic beginning on E, descending

Eb Major, descending

3. Draw a note above each given note to complete the following intervals. Observe the key signatures.

P5   m3   M7   A4   d8   M2   m6   d7

4. Notate each of the following chords.

c ø6/5   f °7   A Maj. 5/3   G Aug. 6/3   Eb°   G Maj. 4/3

E Maj. 6/3   Ab Aug. 5/3   d °4/2   c# °6/4   f# min. 4/2   Cb Dom. 6/5

db min. 6   B Maj. 2   gb min. 6/4   E Dom. 4/3   d half-dim. 7   f min. 7

5. Notate the following secondary dominants and their resolutions.

V⁷/IV   IV6/4   V4/3/ii   ii⁶   V6/5/iii   iii   V4/2/vi   vi⁶

6. Using the Major key, label each of the following chords with its Roman numeral and figured bass.

7. Using the minor key, label each of the following chords with its Roman numeral and figured bass.

8. Write the name for each of the following cadences.

V - I   _____

IV - I   _____

Ends on V   _____

V - VI   _____

LESSON 6: TEXTURE AND COMPOSITIONAL TECHNIQUES

Texture refers to the manner in which the various voices in a musical composition combine to create the sound.

Homophonic Texture refers to music in which one voice dominants, while the other voice or voices are accompaniments. Homophonic texture can be divided into two styles: **Melody with Accompaniment,** and **Chordal Homophony** (sometimes called **Chordal Texture).**

The following example of homophonic texture is a melody with accompaniment.

Mozart: *Sonata, KV 333*

The following example demonstrates chordal homophony (chordal texture).

Schumann: *Grösse Sonata, Op. 14*

Polyphonic or **Contrapuntal** texture contains two or more independent voices. The harmony is created by the blending of the independent voices, as in the following example.

J.S. Bach: *Toccata, BWV 913*

34

A **motive** (or **motif)** is a small musical unit that is the basis of a composition. A motive may be melodic, rhythmic, or harmonic in nature. Occurances of the motive are marked in this example.

Schubert: *Moments Musicaux, Op. 94, No. 2*

A **theme** is a complete musical idea or phrase upon which a musical composition is created. The following example is the theme of the composition.

Schubert: *Impromptu, Op. 90, No. 1*

Repetition: Motive repeated immediately on the same note:

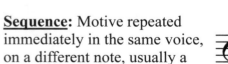

Sequence: Motive repeated immediately in the same voice, on a different note, usually a 2nd or 3rd above or below:

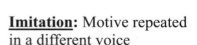

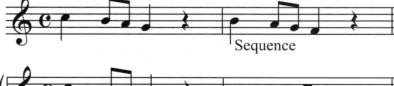

Imitation: Motive repeated in a different voice

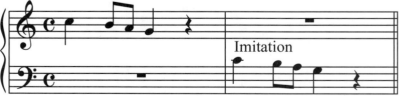

Canon: Repetition of an entire theme or phrase in another voice. The canon may be on the same note, in another octave, or on a different note. Sometimes the intervals are changed slightly for a better sound.

Pedal Point: A sustained note in one voice, usually but not always in the bass:

Ostinato: A persistently repeated pattern:

Augmentation: Rhythmic value of each note is doubled:

Diminution: Rhythmic value of each note is shortened by half:

36

Mark the correct definition for each of the following terms.

1. Ostinato

_____ a. sustained note in one voice
_____ b. persistently repeated pattern
_____ c. exact repetition of entire theme in another voice
_____ d. melody with accompaniment

2. Theme

_____ a. short musical idea that is basis for a composition
_____ b. repetition of motive on a different note in the same voice
_____ c. complete musical idea or phrase that is basis of a composition
_____ d. doubling of rhythmic value of each note

3. Canon

_____ a. exact repetition of entire theme in another voice
_____ b. rhythmic value of each note is cut in half
_____ c. two or more independent voices
_____ d. repetition of motive in a different voice

4. Diminution

_____ a. repetition of motive on a different note in the same voice
_____ b. sustained note in one voice
_____ c. rhythmic value of each note is cut in half
_____ d. short musical idea that is basis for a composition

5. Motive

_____ a. complete musical idea or phrase that is basis for a composition
_____ b. sustained note in one voice
_____ c. exact repetition of an entire theme in another voice
_____ d. short musical idea that is basis of a composition

6. Augmentation

_____ a. doubling of rhythmic value of each note
_____ b. motive repeated immediately on the same note
_____ c. repetition of motive on a different note in the same voice
_____ d. persistently repeated pattern

7. Sequence

_____ a. two or more independent voices
_____ b. repetition of motive on a different note in the same voice
_____ c. melody with accompaniment
_____ d. motive repeated immediately on the same note

8. Homophonic texture

_____ a. melody with accompaniment
_____ b. two or more independent voices
_____ c. rhythmic value of each note is cut in half
_____ d. repetition of motive in a different voice

9. Polyphonic texture
   (Contrapuntal)

_____ a. motive repeated immediately on the same note
_____ b. exact repetition of entire theme in another voice
_____ c. melody with accompaniment
_____ d. two or more independent voices

10. Repetition   _____ a. motive repeated immediately on the same note
       _____ b. short musical idea that is basis of a composition
       _____ c. persistently repeated pattern
       _____ d. two or more independent voices

11. Imitation   _____ a. complete musical idea or phrase that is basis of a composition
       _____ b. sustained note in one voice
       _____ c. repetition of motive in a different voice
       _____ d. rhythmic value of each note is cut in half

12. Pedal point   _____ a. persistently repeated pattern
       _____ b. short musical idea that is basis of a composition
       _____ c. two or more independent voices
       _____ d. sustained note in one voice

Answer questions 13-17 about the above example.

13. Circle the motive on the music.

14. What term is used for the entire melody if   _____
it is the basis of a composition?

15. Name the compositional technique used   a. _____
for each of the labeled items.

                                            b. _____

                                            c. _____

                                            d. _____

16. Does this example contain augmentation?   _____

17. What is the texture of this example?   _____

38

Answer questions 18-20 about the above example.

18. Which of these terms describes the
relationship between the treble clef
and the bass clef?

_____ augmentation
_____ diminution
_____ canon
_____ motive

19. What is the texture of the example?

_____ homophonic
_____ polyphonic

20. Which of these terms may also be used
to describe the texture?

_____ augmentation
_____ contrapuntal

When music is **transposed,** it is written in a key other than the original. To transpose a melody, move every note up or down the same distance, or the same interval. Double check the transposition by making sure all notes have the same intervals that they had in the original when moving from one note to the next. Also look to see if notes that are the same in the original are the same in the transposition, such as all D's becoming E's if transposing up a Major 2nd..

The following melody is transposed from D Major to F Major: Every note is moved up a minor 3rd. All D's become F's, all E's become G's, etc. The intervals from one note to the next remain the same as they were in the original key.

21. Transpose the following melody from the key of G Major to the key of F Major.

LESSON 7: NONHARMONIC TONES

Nonharmonic tones are notes that do not belong in the chords that form the implied harmony. The performance of a nonharmonic tone is called the **Realization.**

Anticipation:* A nonharmonic tone in which the presentation of a chord tone occurs immediately before the actual chord.

Acciaccatura: A keyboard ornament of the late Baroque Period in which a non-chord tone, usually the 2nd or one step below a chord tone, is added to the chord then immediately released.

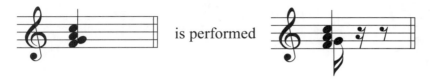

is performed

Appoggiatura:* 1. a nonharmonic tone that is performed at the same time as the chord, followed by a resolution to a chord tone.

2. A melodic ornament with many different realizations in different periods of music history.

    Baroque Period: Notated ♪, the length of an appoggiatura varies depending on the melodic and harmonic structure of the piece. Students of the Baroque Period were taught the guidelines to follow when applying appoggiaturas to music.

    Classical Period: Standardized use of the appoggiatura brought the following guidelines:

If possible, the note is to be divided equally.

is performed

Elements marked * are required for MTAC
Certificate of Merit® Theory Exam

40

Appoggiaturas before dotted notes receive 2/3 of the note value.

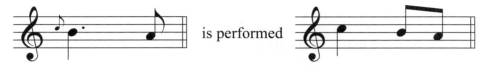 is performed

Appoggiaturas in compound meters receive one full beat.

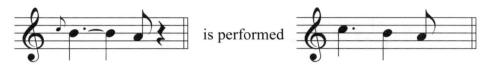 is performed

Appoggiaturas followed by a note then a rest receive the complete value of the note.

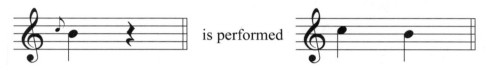 is performed

Under certain circumstances, appoggiaturas are played more quickly, but still on the beat. These include when the appoggiatura is:

With faster notes.

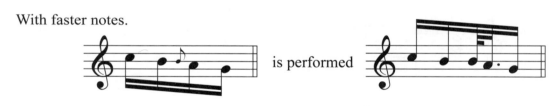 is performed

With repeated notes.

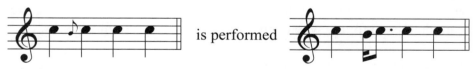 is performed

With syncopated notes.

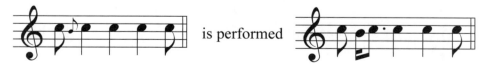 is performed

The information on this page and the first three examples of appoggiaturas on the next page are not required for MTAC Certificate of Merit® Theory Exam

When the main note is a harmonic appoggiatura:

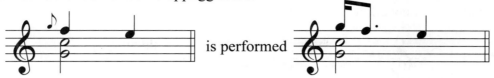

is performed

When the main note is a suspension:

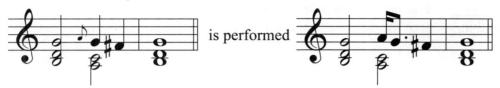

is performed

When the appoggiatura fills in a series of descending thirds:

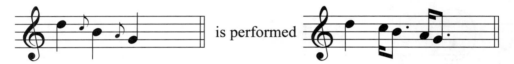

is performed

Neighbor Tone:* A nonharmonic tone which steps below (lower neighbor) or above (upper neighbor) the chord tones, then returns.

               Lower Neighbor   Upper Neighbor

Passing Tone:* A nonharmonic tone which steps between two chords.

Pivot Chord:* A chord that is common to both the original key and the key to which the music modulates. The music must change keys for there to be a pivot chord.

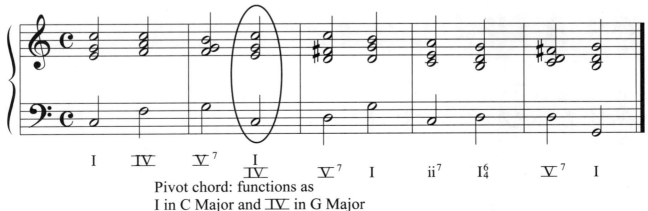

I   IV   V⁷   I   V⁷   I   ii⁷ I⁶₄ V⁷ I

IV

Pivot chord: functions as
I in C Major and IV in G Major

Suspension:* A nonharmonic tone in which the chord tone is held beyond the next chord change, then resolved after the new chord is played.

Tertian Harmony:* Harmonic system based on the third. Tertian harmony is the common harmony used in Western music. Triads and seventh chords are created using tertian harmony.

1. Name the circled element in each of the following examples: Anticipation, Acciaccatura, Appoggiatura, Upper Neighbor, Lower Neighbor, Passing Tone, Pivot Chord, or Suspension.

a. _____

b. _____

c. _____

d. _____

e. _____

f. _____

2. Notate the realization for each of the following examples.

3. Name the circled nonharmonic tone in each of the following examples.

a. From *Sonata, K. 310: Rondo,* by Mozart. _____

b. From *Sonata, Hob. XVI:50: Allegro*, by Haydn. _____

c. From *Sonata, Hob. XVI:49: Finale*, by Haydn. _____

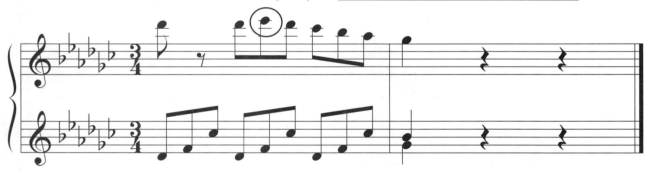

d. From *Sonata, K. 309, Andante un poco Adagio*, by Mozart. _____

e. From *Sonata, K. 311: Allegro con spirito*, by Mozart. _____

f. From *Sonata, L. 58*, by Scarlatti. _____

From *Sonata, K. 311: Allegro con spirito*, by Mozart. _____

Mozart: *Sonata, K. 284: Allegro*

Answer the following questions about the above example.

4. What type of augmented 6th is chord **a**?

     _____ Fr.$^{+6}$

     _____ Ger.$^{+6}$

     _____ It.$^{+6}$

5. What name is used for chord **b**?

     _____ Secondary dominant

     _____ Dominant

     _____ Plagal cadence

6. Define Tertian Harmony. _____

_____

LESSON 8: 20th and 21st CENTURY COMPOSITIONAL DEVICES

Atonality: No specific key, tonality, or mode.

Bitonality: The combination of two keys at the same time (such as E Major and F Major as in the following example). Bitonality is a type of Polytonality.

Melodic Inversion: The process of turning each interval of a melody upside down. For example, a M3 up becomes a M3 down.

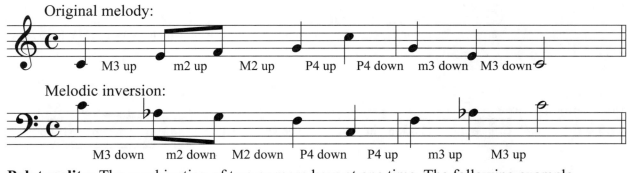

Polytonality: The combination of two or more keys at one time. The following example includes F Major (top voice), D Major (middle voice), and E♭ Major (bass clef). Bitonality is a form of Polytonality.

> **Terminology in this lesson required for MTAC**
> **Certificate of Merit® theory exam**

48

Quartal Harmony: Harmony based on the interval of a fourth.

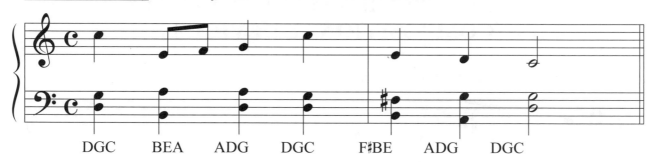

DGC   BEA   ADG   DGC   F♯BE   ADG   DGC

Retrograde: The reversal of a melody, as if reading from right to left.

Original melody:

Retrograde:

Retrograde Inversion: Reversal of a melody as if reading from right to left (retrograde) combined with the melodic inversion of the melody (the inversion of each interval).

Original melody:

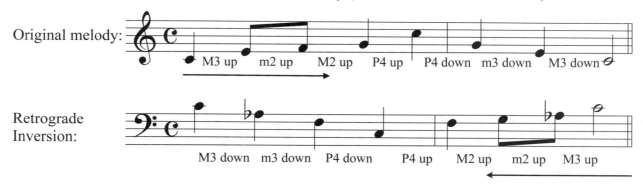

M3 up   m2 up   M2 up   P4 up   P4 down   m3 down   M3 down

Retrograde Inversion:

M3 down   m3 down   P4 down   P4 up   M2 up   m2 up   M3 up

Serialism: Music that is based on a particular succession of pitches, rhythms, dynamics or other elements that are repeated over and over to provide the underlying structure of the composition.

Twelve Tone Row: A melody or series used in Serial music that includes all twelve pitches. The compositional techniques of melodic inversion, retrograde, and retrograde inversion may be strictly adhered to throughout the music.

1. Identify whether each of the following phrases is an example of Atonality, Bitonality, Polytonality, Quartal Harmony, or Twelve Tone Row.

a. _____

b. _____

c. _____

d. _____

e. _____

2. Notate this melody using retrograde for the pitches, but keeping the rhythm the same as in the original melody.

3. Notate this melody using inversion. Keep the original rhythm.

4. Notate this melody using regrograde inversion. Keep the original rhythm.

5. Complete this twelve tone row by notating the three missing pitches. Any order is acceptable.

OPTIONAL, FOR EXTRA STUDY:
ANAYLZING TWELVE-TONE SERIAL MUSIC

To analyze a serial composition that uses a twelve-tone row, a grid can be created that includes all possible versions of the row. The following is a twelve-tone row:

| d5 down | M2 down | M2 down | P4 up | A5 up | A4 down | M2 up | M6 up | A2 down | P5 down | A2 up |

To analyze the composition, an analysis grid is created. The grid will show the series, melodic inversion, retrograde, and retrograde inversion beginning on each of the twelve notes.

To create the grid:

1. List each interval and its direction in the header row. Invert each interval and list them in the left column.
2. Write the note names, including accidentals, from left to right in the top row.
3. Write the melodic inversion in the left column, beginning with the first note of the series. Keep the note names consistent (for example, always use B♭, not A♯).

2. Series ⟶

3. Inversion ↓	1. Intervals	d5 down	M2 down	M2 down	P4 up	A5 up	A4 down	M2 up	M6 up	A2 down	P5 down	A2 up	
		B♭	E	D	C	F	C♯	G	A	F♯	E♭	A♭	B
	d5 up	E											
	M2 up	F♯											
	M2 up	A♭											
	P4 down	E♭											
	A5 down	G											
	A4 up	C♯											
	M2 down	B											
	M6 down	D											
	A2 up	F											
	P5 up	C											
	A2 down	A											

> **Creating an analysis grid is not required for MTAC Certificate of Merit® theory test.**

4. Begin the second horizontal line of the grid. Complete this line by using the same intervals as the series (the top horizontal line of the grid). Double check the line by making sure that:

   a. all twelve notes of the chromatic scale are used, and that there are no missing or duplicate notes.
   b. that the intervals listed in the far left column match the vertical line of note names.

5. Complete the grid by repeating step 4 for each line, remembering to double check for accuracy. When completed, each occurrence of the twelve-tone row in the notated composition can be matched with the grid to determine the type of variation that is used (transposed series, melodic inversion, regrograde, or retrograde inversion). Each note may appear in any octave, and notes may be combined to form chords.

Series ——>   **<—— Retrograde**

	d5 down	M2 down	M2 down	P4 up	A5 up	A4 down	M2 up	M6 up	A2 down	P5 down	A2 up	
d5 up	B♭	E	D	C	F	C♯	G	A	F♯	E♭	A♭	B
M2 up	E	B♭	A♭	F♯	B	G	C♯	E♭	C	A	D	F
M2 up	F♯	C	B♭	A♭	C♯	A	E♭	F	D	B	E	G
P4 down	A♭	D	C	B♭	E♭	B	F	G	E	C♯	F♯	A
A5 down	E♭	A	G	F	B♭	F♯	C	D	B	A♭	C♯	E
A4 up	G	C♯	B	A	D	B♭	E	F♯	E♭	C	F	A♭
M2 down	C♯	G	F	E♭	A♭	E	B♭	C	A	F♯	B	D
M6 down	B	F	E♭	C♯	F♯	D	A♭	B♭	G	E	A	C
A2 up	D	A♭	F♯	E	A	F	B	C♯	B♭	G	C	E♭
P5 up	F	B	A	G	C	A♭	D	E	C♯	B♭	E♭	F♯
A2 down	C	F♯	E	D	G	E♭	A	B	A♭	F	B♭	C♯
	A	E♭	C♯	B	E	C	F♯	A♭	F	D	G	B♭

(Left vertical axis: **Inversion** ↓ ; lower portion: **Retrograde Inversion**)

This example uses the series shown on page 52. The uses of the series are marked on the score.

Series (Row)

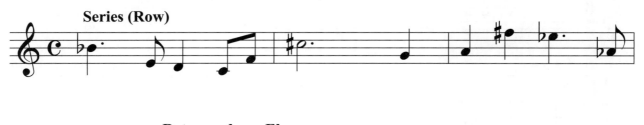

Retrograde on Eb

Inversion on C

Retrograde Inversion on D

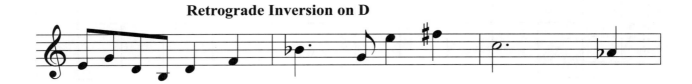

Series on D

54

6. (Optional, for Extra Study): Complete an analysis grid for this series.

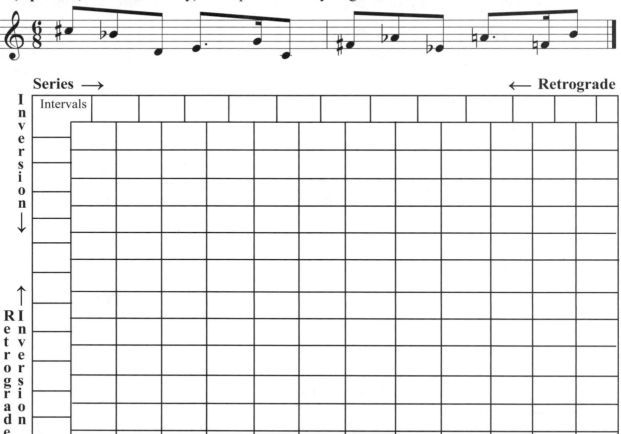

7. (Optional, for Extra Study): Analyze the following example using the grid. Mark each use of the row (series) with the terms series, melodic inversion, retrograde, or retrograde inversion. Write the name of the starting pitch (for example, retrograde on G.)

REVIEW: LESSONS 6-8

1. Each of the following examples is based on the musical idea shown in question a. Write the name of the compositional technique that is used in each example.

a. What term is used for a short musical idea that

is the basis for a composition? _____

b. _____

c. _____

d. _____

e. _____

f. _____

g. _____

h. _____

56

2. Match each of the following terms with its definition.

_____ Homophonic texture

_____ Pedal point

_____ Theme

_____ Polyphonic texture (Contrapuntal)

a. Complete musical idea or phrase on which the composition is based
b. Melody with accompaniment
c. Two independent voices
d. A sustained note in one voice while other voices move

3. Transpose this melody from the key of B♭ Major to the key of D Major.

4. Name the circled nonharmonic tone in each of the following measures.

_____   _____   _____   _____   _____   _____

5. Notate the following melody in the empty measures using retrograde.

6. Notate the following melody in the empty measures using melodic inversion. Begin the third measure on the note A.

7. Write the correct term for each definition.

a. _____ Combination of two or more keys at the same time
b. _____ No specific key, tonality or mode
c. _____ Music based on a series of notes that is repeated over and over
d. _____ Series that includes all notes of the chromatic scale
e. _____ Harmony based on the interval of a third
f. _____ Two different keys at the same time
g. _____ Harmony based on the interval of a fourth
h. _____ Chord that precedes a key change, and is common to both the original key and the new key

LESSON 9: THE FUGUE

The **Fugue** is a style of composition in which 3 or more voices imitate one another. The following terms identify the various components of the fugue.

Subject: The principle theme of the fugue

Answer: A restatement of the subject

Real Answer: An exact transposition of the subject, often to the dominant

Tonal Answer: An answer in which the intervals are adjusted to maintain a sense of the tonality

Countersubject: A distinctive contrapuntal theme that continues in the first voice as the second voice enters and is used repeatedly throughout the fugue

Exposition: The introduction of all voices at the beginning of the fugue; the exposition usually ends with a cadence

Episode: Sections without complete subjects, but that utilize the motivic material from the subject and countersubject

Stretto: Typically found near the end of a fugue, the entrances of the subjects are close together, causing them to overlap. (The term *stretto* is also used in non-fugal music to mean a concluding section which is faster than the preceding music.)

Several terms associated with a fugue are marked in this composition by J. S. Bach. An audio download of this music is available at www.bktmusic.com. Select "Level 10 Audio Files."

Terminology in this lesson required for MTAC Certificate of Merit® theory test

Countersubject

Subject (Tonic)

End of Exposition **EPISODE**

Subject (Relative Major)

Countersubject

EPISODE

Subject

The following assignments are based on the fugue **on the following pages (pp. 63-66).** An audio download of this music is available at www.bktmusic.com. Select "Level 10 Audio Files."

Assignment 1

1. Notate the Subject from the fugue that begins on **page 63**.

2. a. In which measure does the answer begin? _____

   b. Is it a real or tonal answer? _____ Why? _____

   c. Based on the tonal center of the answer (not on the first note of the answer), on which scale degree does this voice occur? _____

3. a. In which measure does the third voice enter? _____

   b. Based on the tonal center of the answer (not on the first note of the answer), on which scale degree does this voice occur? _____

4. a. In which measure does the fourth voice enter? _____

   b. Based on the tonal center of the answer (not on the first note of the answer), on which scale degree does this voice occur? _____

5. Notate the countersubject.

6. Beginning in measure 12, the music briefly passes through several different tonal centers. Name each, and write how they are related to the original key or to one another.

	Name of Key	**Relationship to Tonic or to One Another**
Measure 12	_____	_____
Measure 14	_____	_____
Measure 16 (4th beat)	_____	_____
Measure 20	_____	_____
Measure 24	_____	_____

Assignment 2: Optional, for Extra Study

1. Beginning with measure 12, write the measure number of each entrance of the subject. Reminder: The subject may be adjusted melodically and harmonically.

   a. Measure __12__

   b. Measure ____

   c. Measure ____

   d. Measure ____

   e. Measure ____

   f. Measure ____

   g. Measure ____

   h. Measure ____

   i. Measure ____

   j. Measure ____

   k. Measure ____

   l. Measure ____

   m. Measure ____

2. There are two occurences of *stretto* in this fugue. Write the measure numbers of each.

   a. Measures ____ to ____

   b. Measures ____ to ____

3. Starting at the beginning of the fugue, write the measure number for each entrance of the countersubject.

   a. Measure ____

   b. Measure ____

   c. Measure ____

   d. Measure ____

   e. Measure ____

   f. Measure ____

   g. Measure ____

   h. Measure ____

   i. Measure ____

   j. Measure ____

   k. Measure ____

   l. Measure ____

4. Write the measure numbers for the Exposition. Measures ____ to ____

5. Write the measure numbers for each Episode.

   a. Measures ____ to ____

   b. Measures ____ to ____

   c. Measures ____ to ____

   d. Measures ____ to ____

6. For each of indicated measures, name the key. Label the pair of chords that form the cadence with Roman numerals and figured bass. Write the name of each cadence.

Meas. 11, beat 4 - Meas. 12, beat 1

Key of _____ _____

Roman numerals: _____ _____

Name of Cadence: _____

Meas. 27, beats 3 & 4 - Meas. 28, beat 1

Key of _____ _____

Roman numerals: _____ _____

Name of Cadence: _____

Measure 19, beat 4 - Meas. 20, beat 1

Key of _____ _____

Roman numerals: _____ _____

Name of Cadence: _____

Meas. 34, beats 2-3

Key of _____ _____

Roman numerals: _____ _____ *

Name of Cadence: _____

Measures 24, beats 2-3

Key of _____ _____

Roman numerals: _____ _____

Name of Cadence: _____

*The final cadence has a raised 3rd, causing the chord to be Major instead of minor. This is called a **Picardy Third**.

Fugue, BWV 861, by J.S. Bach

64

LESSON 10: SONATA FORM

A <u>**Sonata**</u> is a composition for piano or other solo instrument that has several separate sections known as <u>**movements**</u>. The movements are usually in different keys and have differing forms. The typical format for the movements of a Classical Sonata are:

<u>**Allegro:**</u> Sonata form (also known as Sonata Allegro form)

<u>**Adagio:**</u> Binary or Ternary form, in a different but closely related to that of the first movement (such as the dominant or relative minor).

<u>**Scherzo**</u> or <u>**Minuet**</u> (optional): Ternary form (Scherzo and Trio or Minuet and Trio), in the same key as the first movement

<u>**Allegro**</u> (or <u>**Presto**</u>): Rondo form or Variations, in the same key as the first movement

This format is not always followed. There are often fewer than four movements (in which case it is usually the Scherzo/Minuet movement that is missing), or a Sonata may begin with a slow movement rather than a fast movement.

The first movement of a Sonata is usually in <u>**Sonata**</u> form. There are three sections:

<u>**EXPOSITION**</u>: **Theme 1** (Tonic key)   **Bridge**   **Theme 2** (Dominant or other related key)

<u>**DEVELOPMENT**</u>:   Motives based on Themes 1 and 2 are developed in various keys

<u>**RECAPITULATION**</u>: **Theme 1** (Tonic key)   **Bridge**   **Theme 2** (Tonic key)

The Exposition is typically repeated, and the Development and Recapitulation are repeated together.

The first movement of *Sonata, XVI:27* by Haydn is shown below. The sections, themes, and keys are marked. The second movement of this sonata (not included) is a Minuet and Trio in the key of G Major (Tonic). The third movement (not included) is a Rondo in the key of G Major (Tonic). An audio download of this music is available at www.bktmusic.com. Select "Level 10 Audio Files."

EXPOSITION
          Theme 1 (G Major, I)

> **Sonata form and tempos and forms of the various movements**
> **are required for MTAC Certificate of Merit® theory exam**

DEVELOPMENT
(Various keys)

RECAPITULATION
Theme 1 (G Major, I)

Bridge (Different from Exposition)

Theme 2 (G Major, I)

Answer these questions about *Sonata, K. 280: Allegro assai*, by Mozart, which follows on pages **74-82**. An audio download of this music is available at www.bktmusic.com. Select "Level 10 Audio Files."

Assignment 1 (Music on Pages 74-82)

1. Mark the beginning of the Exposition, Development, and Recapitulation on the music for the Sonata on pages 74-82.

2. Mark Theme 1, the Bridge, and Theme 2 in the Exposition and Recapitulation.

3. Determine the key in which each section and each theme begins. Mark the keys on the music.

4. Complete the following chart.

	Exposition		Development		Recapitulation	
	Theme 1	Theme 2	Begins in	Ends in	Theme 1	Theme 2
Key of:						
Relationship to Tonic:						

Assignment 2 (Optional, for Extra Study)

1. Complete a harmonic analysis of the music. Write the Roman Numerals and figured bass on the lines below the staff. If the line has parenthesis (___ _____), label the chord with its root, quality, and figured bass.

Assignment 3 (Optional, for Extra Study)

1. Write the name of each cadence where indicated.

2. Locate and mark these compositional techniques found in the music: **sequence, pedal point, syncopation, repetition, and imitation.**

3. Carefully compare the Exposition and Recapitulation. List some of the differences.

_____

_____

_____

4. a. Name the circled nonharmonic tone in measure 6. _____

   b. Name the circled nonharmonic tone in measure 64. _____

74

Allegro assai

cadence

cadence   New key: ___ _____

cadence

_____ cadence

New key: ____ Major

cadence

80

cadence

_____ cadence

LESSON 11: RONDO FORM

Rondo Form, which is often used for the final movement of a sonata, is a form in which one section (usually the first section) is repeated several times with contrasting sections between, creating a form such as:

A   B   A   C   A

It is most typical for the A sections to be in the tonic key and the contrasting sections to be in keys other than tonic.

The form and the key for each section of the following Rondo, the final movement of *Sonata, Hob. XVI:48* by Haydn, is below. An audio download of this music is available at www.bktmusic.com. Select "Level 10 Audio Files."

A	B	A	C	A	D
C Major (I)	G Major (V̲)	G Major (V̲)	G Major (V̲)	C Major (I)	c minor (i)

A	B	A	C	Coda (Based on A)
C Major (I)	C Major (I)	C Major (I)	C Major (I)	C Major (I)

**Understanding of Rondo Form required for
MTAC Certificate of Merit® theory exam**

84

B (C then G Major)

A (G Major)

C (G Major)

A (C Major)

D (c minor)

A (C Major)

B (C then G Major)

A (C Major)

94

C (C Major)

95

Coda (C Major)

Answer these questions about the Rondo on **pages 97-106** from *Sonata, K. 281* by Mozart. An audio download of this music is available at www.bktmusic.com. Select "Level 10 Audio Files."

Assignment 1 (Music on Pages 97-106)

1. a. Mark the sections of the music **on pages 97-106** using capital letters (A, B, etc.).

   b. Fill in the following chart with the letter, key, and relationship to tonic for each section. The first row is given.

Name of Section	Key	Relationship to Tonic
A	B-flat Major	I - Tonic

Assignment 2

1. Compare the A sections with one another. List some differences.

_____

_____

_____

_____

2. Compare the B sections with one another. List some differences.

_____

_____

_____

3. Name the nonharmonic tone that is circled in each of the following measures.

   Measure 3 _____   Measure 55 _____

   Measure 12 _____   Measure 59 _____

   Measure 38 _____   Measure 91 _____

4. What type of chord is circled in measure 62? _____

Assignment 3 (Optional, for Extra Study)

1. Complete a harmonic analysis of the music.

- Label each underlined chord with its Roman numeral and figured bass.
- When there is a key change, analyze the chords in the new key.
- For chords with (__ _____), write the root, quality and figured bass.
- Include bass clef notes that are held beyond a chord change in the analysis.
- Long lines under a chord indicate that more notes are to be included.

Assignment 4 (Optional, for Extra Study)

1. Name each of the marked cadences.

2. Find the following compositional techniques that appear in the music and mark them on the score: **Repetition, Imitation, Sequence**.

cadence

New key ___ ____: ___ (Pivot chord)

New key: ___ ___ ___ ___ (Pivot chord)

New key: _____ _____

_____ cadence

_____ cadence

_____ cadence

cadence

New key: ___ ___

84

87

90

New key: _____ _____

93

96

99

_____ cadence

____ (pivot chord)

New key: ___ _____   _____ cadence

_____ cadence

LESSON 12: THEME AND VARIATIONS

Theme and Variations (or **Variation Form**) is a form in which a theme is presented, then repeated with changes to the melody, harmony, rhythm, form, texture, key, mode, meter, or tempo. Typically, these changes are made without completely hiding the original theme.

Study this Theme and Variations, *Mio caro Adone aus Saleiri's "La fiera di Venezia,"* by Mozart. An audio download of this music is available at www.bktmusic.com. Select "Level 10 Audio Files." The basic changes are:

Theme: Key of G Major
Variation 1: Key of G Major, melody uses eighth notes.
Variation 2: Key of G Major, melody uses triplets.
Variation 3: Key of G Major, melody uses sixteenths.
Variation 4: Key of G Major, melody uses trills, syncopation, octaves, and sixteenths.
Variation 5: Key of G Major, uses 32nds in left hand accompaniment, slower tempo.
Variation 6: Key of G Major, duple meter, faster tempo, sixteenths, rolled chords.

Theme: Andante

┌───┐
│ **Understanding of Theme and Variations required for** │
│ **MTAC Certificate of Merit® theory test** │
└───┘

Variation 1

Variation 2

Variation 3

Variation 4

Variation 5

Adagio

Variation 6

Adagio

Answer these questions about this Theme and Variations (*Variation No. 15 on an Allegretto*) by Mozart, on **pages 115-122.** An audio download of this music is available at www.bktmusic.com. Select "Level 10 Audio Files."

1. Analyze the **Theme** harmonically (**page 115-116**). Write the Roman numerals and figured bass on the lines below each staff.

2. Briefly describe the changes in Variation 1. _____

   Does the key change? _____ Does the basic harmony change? _____

3. Briefly describe the changes in Variation 2. _____

   Does the key change? _____ Does the basic harmony change? _____

4. Briefly describe the changes in Variation 3. _____

   Does the key change? _____ Does the basic harmony change? _____

5. Briefly describe the changes in Variation 4. _____

   Does the key change? _____ Does the basic harmony change? _____

6. Briefly describe the changes in Variation 5. _____

   Does the key change? _____ Does the basic harmony change? _____

7. Briefly describe the changes in Variation 6. _____

   Does the key change? _____ Does the basic harmony change? _____

8. Briefly describe the changes in the Coda. _____

9. Name the circled nonharmonic tones in each of the following measures.

Meas. 1 _____ Meas. 2 _____ Meas. 4 _____ Meas. 10 _____

Meas. 32 _____ Meas. 33 _____ Meas. 81 _____

Theme
Allegretto

F Major: ___ ___   ___ ___ ___   ___ ___ ___ ___

5

C Major: ___

9

12

___ F Major: ___

Variation 1

17

19

22

Variation 2

Variation 3

Variation 4

Variation 5

Variation 6

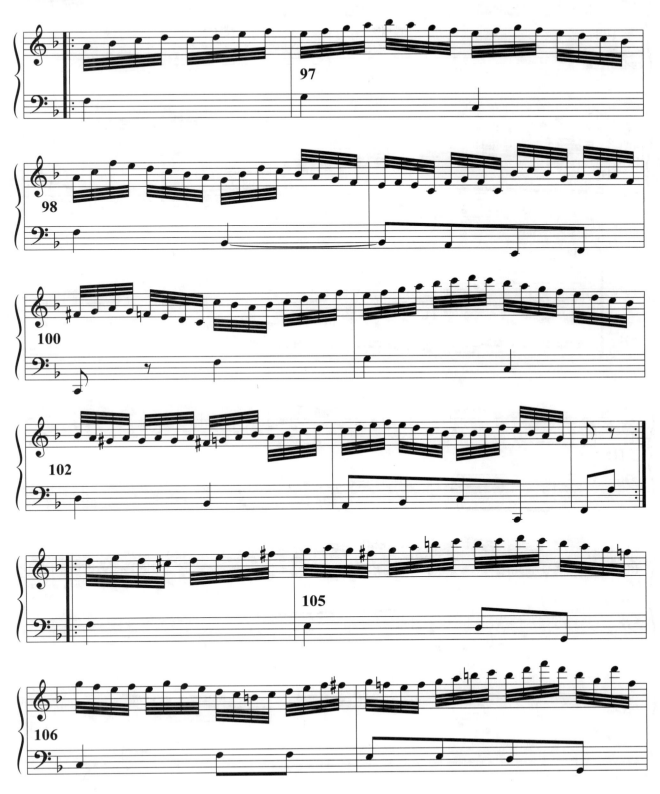

LESSON 13: TERMINOLOGY AND MUSIC HISTORY OVERVIEW

The history of music since 1600 is typically divided into the following periods.

Baroque Period: 1600-1750

Characteristics	Composers
Polyphonic texture	J.S. Bach
Use of ornamentation	Corelli
Improvisation	Handel
Use of figured bass	Rameau
Dance Suite	Scarlatti
Keyboard instruments: Harpsichord, Clavichord, Organ	Telemann
	Vivaldi
Terraced Dynamics (*p mp mf f*)	

Classical Period: 1750-1830

Characteristics	Composers
Homophonic texture	Beethoven*
Obvious cadence points	Clementi
Alberti bass	Czerny
Sonata form	Diabelli
	Haydn
	Kuhlau
	Mozart

Romantic Period: 1830-1900

Characteristics	Composers	
Programme music (about things, people, places, etc.)	Brahms	Mendelssohn
Descriptive titles	Chopin	Schubert
Colorful harmonies and chromaticism	Dvořák	Schumann
Lyric melodies	Grieg	Tchaikovsky
Complex rhythmic patterns	Liszt	

*Beethoven is considered a transitional composer between Classical and Romantic

Impressionism

Impressionism is a style of composition in the late 19th century, inspired by the Impressionistic movement in art.

Characteristics	Composers
Unresolved dissonances	Debussy
Nonharmonic tones added to triads	Griffes
Parallel motion	Ravel
Whole-tone and pentatonic scales	
Irregular phrasing	

20th and 21st Centuries (Contemporary): 1900-Present

Currently, there is not a definitive division of years for the 20th and 21st centuries. Many historians place the Contemporary Period later, beginning after 1950 or 1960. This period may also be called Modern or Post-Common Practice. Another division is the 20th Century (1900-1999), and the Contemporary Period (2000-Present).

Characteristics	Composers	
Less use of major and minor tonalities	Bartók	Kabalevsky
Quartal harmony, Bitonality, Polytonality, Atonality	Britten	Poulenc
Irregular and changing meters	Copland	Prokofiev
Polyphonic texture	Dello Joio	Shostakovich
Neo-Classic writing (return to Classical forms)		
Serial music and Twelve-tone music		

1. Name the historical period for each of the following characteristics and composers.

a. _____ Bartók

b. _____ Use of ornamentation

c. _____ Progamme music

d. _____ Clementi

e. _____ Irregular and changing meters

f. _____ Diabelli

g. _____ Brahms

h. _____ Colorful harmonies

i. _____ Terraced dynamics

j. _____ Sonata form

k. _____ Neo-Classic writing

l. _____ Atonality

m. _____ Copland

n. _____ Use of figured bass

o. _____ Britten

p. _____ Tchaikovsky

q. _____ Irregular meters

r. _____ Improvisation

s. _____ Chopin

t. _____ Haydn

u. _____ Prokofiev

v. _____ Quartal harmony

w. _____ Alberti bass

x. _____ Corelli

y. _____ Dello Joio

z. _____ Schubert

TERMINOLOGY

a tempo: return to the original tempo

accelerando: accelerate; gradually faster

accidental: a sharp, flat or natural written before a note

adagio: slowly

allargando: broadening; gradually slower

allegro: fast, quick, cheerfully, merrily

allegretto: slighly slower than Allegro; faster than Andante

andante: walking tempo

andantino: slightly faster than *andante*. (Some composers use it to mean slower than *andante*)

animato: animated; with spirit

articulation: the manner in which notes are executed, including, but not limited to, staccato and legato

arpeggio: notes of a chord played in succession (broken)

cantabile: in a singing style

coda: an extended ending

codetta: a coda at the end of an exposition

con: with

con brio: with vigor or spirit (with brilliance)

con fuoco: With fire or fury

con moto: With motion

crescendo: Gradually louder

D.C. al fine: Go back to the beginning of the piece, and play until the word *fine*

damper pedal: the piano pedal located on the right, used for sustaining the notes

decrescendo or *diminuendo:* gradually softer

dolce: sweetly

doloroso: sadly; sorrowfully

enharmonic: two different names for the same pitch, such as C# and Db

espressivo: expressively

fine: the end

f forte: loud

$f\!f$ fortissimo: very loud

$f\!f\!f$ fortississimo: very, very loud

$f\!p$ forte-piano: loud followed immediately by soft

⌢   fermata: hold the note longer than its value

giocoso: merrily, with humor

gracioso: gracefully

hemiola: a shift of the rhythmic pulse from a division of 2 to a division of 3

largo: very slowly; "large"

legato: connected

leggiero: lightly, delicately

lento: slowly

m.d. mano destra: use the right hand

m.s.: mano sinistra: use the left hand

marcato: Stressed, marked

meno: less

meno mosso: less motion; slower

$m\!f$ mezzo forte: medium loud

$m\!p$ mezzo piano: medium soft

moderato: a moderate or medium tempo

molto: much; very

Opus: A word used to indicate the chronological order in which a composer's music was written

Parallel Major/minor: Major and minor keys with the same letter names (such as C Major and c minor)

p   piano: soft

pp   pianissimo: very soft

ppp   pianississimo: very, very soft

pesante: heavily

Phrase: a musical sentence, often four measures long

piu: more

piu mosso: more motion; faster

poco: little

presto: very fast

rallentando: gradually slower

Relative Major and minor: Major and minor keys which have the same key signature

ritardando (ritard., rit.,): slow down gradually

ritenuto: immediately slower

robusto: robustly, boldly

rubato: "robbed time;" the practice of varying the rhythm of a phrase by slowing or rushing the music

scherzando: playfully, jokingly

sempre: always

senza: without

sf fz sfz   *sforzando:* A sudden, sharp accent

smorzando: dying away

simile: continue in the same style

spiritoso: spirited; with spirit

sostenuto: sustained

sotto voce: in a low voice

staccato: play crisply or detached

subito: suddenly; at once.

syncopation: a momentary contradiction of the meter, such as ♪ ♩ ♪

tempo: the speed at which to play the music

tenuto: hold the note for its full value; may also mean to play the note with a slight accent

toccata: a virtuoso piece common during the Baroque Period, written in free style with many scales and rapid passages.

tranquillo: tranquilly, peacefully, calmly

tre corde: release the una corda pedal (soft pedal; left pedal)

una corda (U.C.): press the left or soft pedal

vivace: quick, lively

vivo: brisk, lively

2. Define these terms.

a. articulation _____

b. accidental _____

c. hemiola _____

d. *leggiero* _____

e. *rubato* _____

f. *scherzando* _____

g. **sf** _____

h. *smorzando* _____

i. *sotto voce* _____

j. syncopation _____

k. toccata _____

l. *senza* _____

REVIEW: LESSONS 9-13

1. Write the correct term for each of the following definitions.

a. _____ The main melody of a fugue

b. _____ A composition that is made up of a theme, followed by different versions of the original theme.

c. _____ The first section of the first movement of a composition in Sonata form

d. _____ The restatement of the subject in a fugue

e. _____ Sections in a fugue without subjects, but that utilize the motivic material from the subject and countersubject

f. _____ The last section of the first movement of a Sonata

g. _____ The two melodies that are often present in the first movement of a composition in Sonata form

h. _____ The exact transposition of the subject of a fugue

i. _____ A distinctive contrapuntal theme that continues in the first voice as the second voice enters, and is used repeatedly throughout the fugue.

j. _____ Usually used near the end of a fugue, a musical passage in which the entrances of the subjects are very close together or overlap

k. _____ The middle section of the first movement of a composition in Sonata form

l. _____ In a fugue, an answer that has been adjusted to maintain a sense of the tonality

m. _____ ABACABA

2. Mark the most likely set of tempos for a three movement Sonata.

_____ Allegro	_____ Largo	_____ Allegretto	_____ Allegro
Andante	Allegro	Lento	Andante
Lento	Vivace	Largo	Vivace

3. Name three composers and two characteristics for each of the following historical periods.

Baroque

Composers: 1. _____   2. _____   3. _____

Characteristics: 1. _____

2. _____

Classical

Composers: 1. _____   2. _____   3. _____

Characteristics: 1. _____

2. _____

Romantic

Composers: 1. _____   2. _____   3. _____

Characteristics: 1. _____

2. _____

Impressionism

Composers: 1. _____   2. _____   3. _____

Characteristics: 1. _____

2. _____

20th and 21st Centuries (Contemporary)

Composers: 1. _____   2. _____   3. _____

Characteristics: 1. _____

2. _____

4. Define these terms.

a. *tenuto*   _____

b. *sostenuto*   _____

c. *ritenuto*   _____

d. *rallentando* _____

e. Opus   _____

f. *giocoso*   _____

Perfect Score: 151
Passing Score (70%): 105

FINAL TEST

1. Notate each of the following key signatures in both clefs. (12 points)

E♭ Major	d minor	e♭ minor	b minor	G♭ Major	B♭ Major

F Major	G Major	f♯ minor	e minor	F♯ Major	C♭ Major

2. Notate each of the following scales or modes using accidentals, not key signatures. (6 points)

f minor, melodic form, ascending and descending

Mixolydian mode beginning on C, ascending

c minor, harmonic form, ascending

Whole tone beginning on G, descending

Chromatic beginning on D, ascending

C♭ Major, ascending

3. Draw a note above each given note to complete the following intervals. Observe the key signature. (8 points)

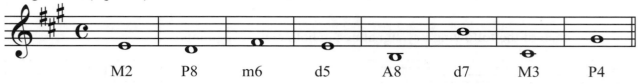

M2   P8   m6   d5   A8   d7   M3   P4

4. Using whole notes, notate each of the following chords. (18 points)

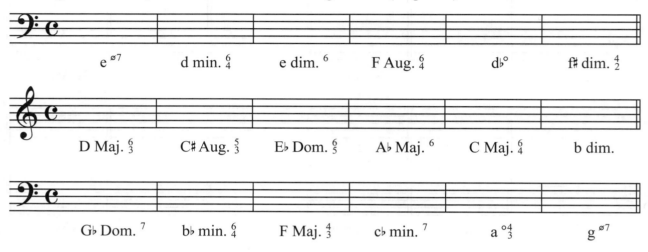

e ⌀7   d min. $\frac{6}{4}$ e dim. 6   F Aug. $\frac{6}{4}$ d♭°   f♯ dim. $\frac{4}{2}$

D Maj. $\frac{6}{3}$ C♯ Aug. $\frac{5}{3}$ E♭ Dom. $\frac{6}{5}$ A♭ Maj. 6   C Maj. $\frac{6}{4}$ b dim.

G♭ Dom. 7   b♭ min. $\frac{6}{4}$ F Maj. $\frac{4}{3}$ c♭ min. 7   a °$\frac{4}{3}$ g ⌀7

5. Using half notes, notate the following secondary dominants and their resolutions. (4 points)

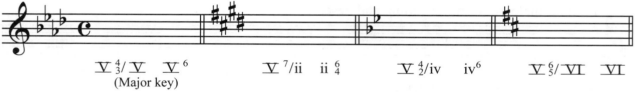

V $\frac{4}{3}$/V V 6   V 7/ii ii $\frac{6}{4}$ V $\frac{4}{2}$/iv iv⁶   V $\frac{6}{5}$/VI VI
(Major key)

6. Using the Major key, label each of the following chords with its Roman numeral and figured bass. (6 points)

_____   _____   _____   _____   _____   _____

7. Using the minor key, label each of the following chords with its Roman numeral and figured bass. (6 points)

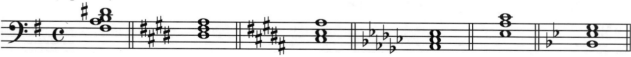

_____   _____   _____   _____   _____   _____

8. Write the name, not the Roman numerals, for each of the following cadences. (4 points)

_____   _____   _____   _____

9. Select the term from the list in the box for each of the following definitions. Not all the terms will be used. (17 points)

a. _____ Music based on a melodic, rhythmic or harmonic idea that is repeated over and over

b. _____ A chord that is common to the original key and the key to which it modulates

c. _____ Melody with accompaniment

d. _____ A long sustained tone over which other notes are moving

e. _____ Repetition of a phrase with the rhythmic value of each note doubled

f. _____ Harmony based on the interval of a fourth

g. _____ A short musical idea that is the basis for a composition

h. _____ A melody with all twelve notes of the chromatic scale that is used as the basis of a composition

i. _____ Harmony based on the interval of a third

j. _____ A persistently repeated pattern

k. _____ A melodic phrase that is the basis of a composition

l. _____ The use of several different keys at the same time

m. _____ Two or more independent melodies that are performed simultaneously

n. _____ Repetition of a phrase with the rhythmic value of each note cut in half

o. _____ No specific key of tonality

p. _____ The exact repetition of an entire melody in a different voice

q. _____ Two different keys or tonalities at the same time

Terms

Homophonic texture

Polyphonic texture

Motive

Theme

Repetition

Sequence

Imitation

Canon

Pedal point

Ostinato

Augmentation

Diminution

Modulation

Pivot chord

Atonality

Bitonality

Polytonality

Quartal harmony

Tertian harmony

Serialism

Twelve-tone row

134

10. Transpose this example from the key of A Major to the key of E♭ Major. (1 point)

11. Notate the following example using retrograde. (1 point)

12. Mark the compositional technique used in the following example. (1 point)

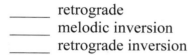

_____ retrograde
_____ melodic inversion
_____ retrograde inversion

13. Name each circled nonharmonic tone in the following phrase. (4 points)

_____   _____   _____   _____

14. Name the historical periods (include Impressionism) in the correct order. Name two composers and two characteristics from each. (25 points)

Historical Period	Composers	Characteristics

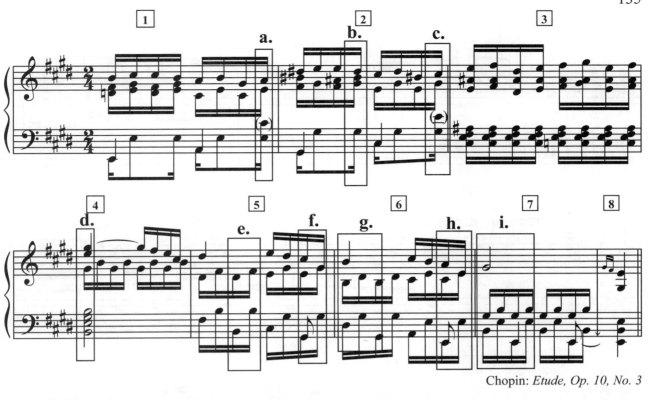

Chopin: *Etude, Op. 10, No. 3*

Answer the following questions about the above example. (16 points)

15. According to the key signature, what is the Major key? _____

16. Name each boxed chord with its Roman numeral and figured bass.

a. _____
b. _____
c. _____
d. _____
e. _____
f. _____
g. _____
h. _____
i. _____

17. Chords **h** and **i** form a cadence. What is the name for this cadence? _____

18. What term describes the rhythm in measure 1, bass clef? _____

19. Compare the melody in measure 1 with the melody in measure 2. What compositional technique is used? _____

20. Write the complete name of the two accidentals that appear in measure 3, bass clef. _____

21. What is the texture of this example? _____

22. Which historical period does Chopin represent? _____

136

J.S. Bach: *Fugue, BWV 858*

Answer these questions about the fugue on page 136. (12 points)

23. What is the key? _____

24. How many voices does this fugue have? _____

25. Notate the subject on the staff below.

26. In what measure does answer enter? _____

27. Based on the tonal center of the answer (not on the first
note of the answer), on which scale degree does the answer
occur? _____

28. Is it a real or tonal answer? _____

29. In what measure does the third voice enter? _____

30. Based on the tonal center of the answer (not on the first
note of the answer), on which scale degree does the third
voice occur? _____

31. This example is from the first section of the fugue, in which
all the voices are introduced. What name is used for this
section? _____

32. What name is used for a section of the fugue in which motivic
material employs various compositional techniques such as
repetition, sequence, diminution, and augmentation? _____

33. What term is used for a section of the fugue in which the
subjects overlap? _____

34. What term is used for a distinctive contrapuntal theme
that continues in the first voice as the second voice
enters with the answer? _____

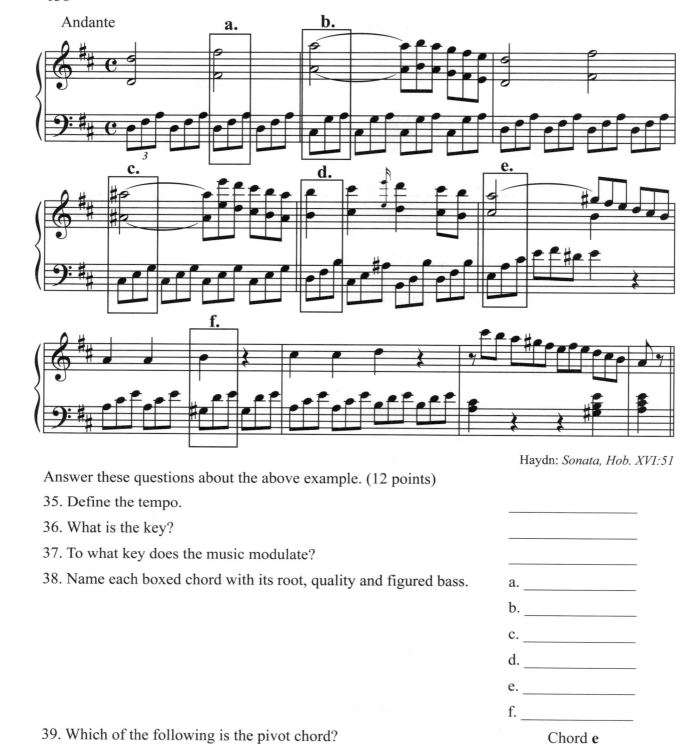

Haydn: *Sonata, Hob. XVI:51*

Answer these questions about the above example. (12 points)

35. Define the tempo. _____

36. What is the key? _____

37. To what key does the music modulate? _____

38. Name each boxed chord with its root, quality and figured bass.

a. _____

b. _____

c. _____

d. _____

e. _____

f. _____

39. Which of the following is the pivot chord?

_____ Chord **e**

_____ Chord **f**

40. This excerpt is from the first movement of the sonata. In the correct order, name the three sections of Sonata form.

_____

_____

_____

41. Would the final movement most likely be a slow tempo or a fast tempo? _____

Glossary

Acciaccatura: A keyboard ornament of the Baroque Period in which a nonharmonic tone, usually the 2nd or one step below a chord tone, is added to the chord then immediately released (Lesson 7)

*Answer: A restatement of the subject in a Fugue (Lesson 9)

*Anticipation: The presentation of a harmonic tone immediately before the actual chord

*Appoggiatura: A nonharmonic tone that is performed with the chord, then resolved to a chord tone (Lesson 7)

*Atonality: No specific key, tonality, or mode used (Lesson 8)

Augmented 6th Chord: An altered chord built on the flatted 6th of the key (the flatted submediant) with the interval of an augmented 6th above the root (Lesson 5)

*Bitonality: The combination of two keys at the same time (Lesson 8)

*Countersubject: In a fugue, a continuation of the subject, which is used repeatedly throughout the fugue (Lesson 9)

*Development: The middle section of Sonata form (Lesson 10)

*Episode: Sections of a fugue without the subject (Lesson 9)

*Exposition: a) In a fugue, the first section in which all voices are introduced (Lesson 9)

b) In a sonata, the first section of Sonata form (Lesson 10)

French 6th: An augmented 6th chord which has four different notes, the intervals being a M3, A4, and A6 above the root (Lesson 5)

*Fugue: A style of composition in which three or more voices enter in imitation of one another (Lesson 9)

German 6th: An augmented 6th chord which has four different notes, the intervals being a M3, P5, and A6 above the root (Lesson 5)

Italian 6th: An augmented 6th chord which contains three notes, the intervals being a M3 and A6 above the root (Lesson 5)

*Required for Certificate of Merit® Theory Exam

*Melodic inversion: The process of turning a melody upside down by intervals (M3 up becomes M3 down, for example) (Lesson 8)

*Passing Tone: A nonharmonic tone which steps between two different chords (Lesson 7)

*Pivot chord: A chord that precedes a modulation, which is common to both the original key and the new key (Lesson 7)

*Polytonality: The combination of several different keys at one time (Lesson 8)

*Real Answer: An exact transposition of a fugue's subject to the dominant (Lesson 9)

*Quartal Harmony: Harmonic system based on the interval of the 4th (Lesson 8)

*Recapitulation: The third section of Sonata form (Lesson 10)

*Retrograde: The reversal of a melody, as if reading from right to left (Lesson 8)

*Regrograde Inversion: The reversal of a melody as if reading from right to left (retrograde), combined with the melodic inversion of the melody (the inversion of each interval) (Lesson 8)

*Rondo: A form in which one section is repeated several times, with contrasting sections between (ABACA) (Lesson 11)

*Row: See Twelve Tone Row (Lesson 8)

*Serialism: Compositional technique in which a series of notes, rhythms, or harmonies are used repeatedly throughout the composition (Lesson 8)

*Series: See Twelve Tone Row (Lesson 8)

*Sonata Form (Sonata Allegro Form): Common form a multiple movement composition, in which the first movement contains three sections: Exposition, Development, and Recapitulation (Lesson 10)

*_stretto_: In a fugue, a term indicating that the entrances of the subjects are close together, causing the subjects to overlap (Lesson 9)

*Subject: The principle theme of a fugue. (Lesson 9)

*Suspension: A nonharmonic tone which is held when the chord changes, then resolved after the new chord is played. (Lesson 7)

*Required for Certificate of Merit® Theory Exam

*Tertian Harmony: Harmonic system based on the interval of the third. (Lesson 7)

*Theme and Variations (Variation Form): A form in which a theme is presented, then repeated with changes to the melody, harmony, rhythm, form, texture, key, mode, meter, or tempo. Typically, these changes are made without completely hiding the original theme (Lesson 12)

*Tonal Answer: In a fugue, an answer in which the transposition is altered slightly (Lesson 9)

*Twelve Tone Row: Melody or series used in serial music in which all twelve notes of the chromatic scale are included (Lesson 8)

*Tone Row: See Twelve Tone Row (Lesson 8)

 *Variation Form: See Theme and Variations (Lesson 12)

This page has purposely been left blank

ANSWER KEY

LESSON 1: KEYS AND SCALES (Pages 1-4)

<u>Page 2</u> No. 1:

BM   b♭m   C♯M   G♭M   a♭m   fm   DM   E♭M

2. Chromatic on F

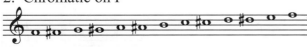

g♯ melodic minor

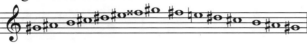

Chromatic on G

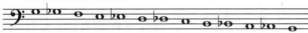

b harmonic minor

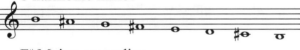

F♯ Major, ascending

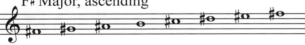

B Major

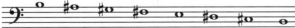

Whole tone on A

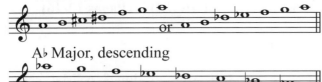

A♭ Major, descending

<u>Page 3</u> No. 3

m2, P4, d8, d7, m6, M3, d6, d5

4.

M6   m7   A4   M2   d4   A2   P5   m3

<u>Page 3, cont.</u>

  5. f♯ minor
  6. f♯ harmonic minor
  7. a. M2
     b. m3
     c. P4
     d. m2
     e. P5

<u>Page 4</u>

  8. E♭ Major
  9. B♭ Major
10. a. P8
     b. M3
     c. P8
     d. m2
     e. M2

11. F
12. T
13. T
14. F
15. F
16. T

LESSON 2: MODES (Pages 5-12)

<u>Page 7</u>

1. (Given)

2. a. D♯, F♯, G♯, C♯, (D♯)
     b. F♯, C♯, G♯, D♯
     c. E Major
     d. 7
     e. Locrian

3. a. B♭
     b. B♭
     c. F
     d. 1
     e. Ionian

Page 7, cont.

4. a. C#, F#
   b. F#, C#
   c. D Major
   d. 4
   e. Lydian

Page 8

5. a. Mixolydian
   b. Phrygian
   c. Aeolian
   d. Lydian
   e. Locrian
   f. Mixolydian
   g. Ionian
   h. Dorian

Page 10

6. (Given)

7. a. P1
   b. F# Major
   c. F#, C#, G#, D#, A#, E#

8. a. M3
   b. C Major
   c. No sharps or flats

9. a. P4
   b. E♭ Major
   c. B♭, E♭, A♭

10. a. M7
    b. C♭ Major
    c. B♭, E♭, A♭, D♭, G♭, C♭, F♭

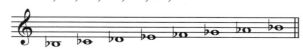

Page 11 No. 11

a.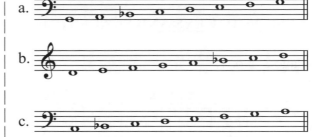

b.

c.

d.

e.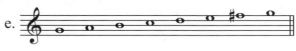

f.

g.

h.

Page 12

12. a. Dorian mode
    b. Mixolydian mode
    c. Lydian mode

LESSON 3: CHORDS (Pages 13-16)

Page 13

1. c min. $\frac{4}{3}$, E♭ Aug. $\frac{6}{4}$, d dim. $\frac{6}{5}$, A♭ Maj. $\frac{6}{3}$,

   e dim. $\frac{4}{3}$, D♭ Aug. $\frac{5}{3}$

   F# Major $\frac{5}{3}$, G♭ Dom. ^{7}, c# min. $\frac{6}{3}$,

   b half dim. $\frac{4}{3}$, G Maj. $\frac{6}{4}$, b♭ min. $\frac{5}{3}$

Page 14, No. 2

DM $\frac{6}{5}$ g♭°⁶   A⁺⁶₄   a♭ m $\frac{5}{3}$ E Dom$\frac{4}{3}$ f♯ °⁶

a⁰⁷   C♭ M $\frac{6}{5}$ f °⁶₄   c♯ m $\frac{4}{2}$ B♭ Dom$\frac{4}{3}$ E♭ M⁷

3. IV$\frac{6}{3}$ ii$\frac{6}{3}$ vi$\frac{6}{4}$ V$\frac{5}{3}$ iii$\frac{5}{3}$ I$\frac{6}{4}$

vii°$\frac{5}{3}$ V$\frac{6}{5}$ iii$\frac{6}{4}$ vii°$\frac{6}{3}$ V$\frac{4}{3}$ ii$\frac{5}{3}$

Page 15, No. 4

ii°   iv⁶   VI   i$\frac{6}{4}$ V⁷   VI$\frac{6}{3}$

vii°   V   V$\frac{4}{2}$ VI$\frac{6}{4}$ ii°   iv$\frac{6}{4}$

5. E♭ Major

6. a. G Major $\frac{5}{3}$

   b. G Dominant $\frac{6}{5}$

   c. C Major $\frac{6}{4}$

   d. A♭ Major $\frac{6}{3}$

   e. E♭ Dominant $\frac{4}{2}$

7. f. V⁷

   g. I $\frac{5}{3}$

   h. ii $\frac{5}{3}$

Page 16

8. D♭ Major

9. a. I$\frac{5}{3}$

   b. IV$\frac{5}{3}$

   c. V⁷

   d. iii$\frac{6}{3}$

   e. I$\frac{5}{3}$

Page 16, cont.

10. 1. d half dim. $\frac{4}{3}$

    2. e dim. $\frac{4}{2}$

    3. A♭ Dom. ⁷

LESSON 4: THE SECONDARY DOMINANT (Pages 17-22)

Page 18

1. a. G♭ Major
   c. F

   V⁷   iii$\frac{6}{4}$

2. a. G Major
   c. E

   V/ii   ii$\frac{6}{4}$

3. a. c♯ minor
   c. E

   V$\frac{6}{5}$/VI   VI

4. a. b minor
   b. B

   V$\frac{6}{5}$/iv   iv

Page 19, No. 2

V$\frac{4}{3}$/IV IV⁶   V⁷/ii ii$\frac{6}{4}$ V$\frac{4}{3}$/ii ii⁶   V⁷/IV IV$\frac{6}{4}$

V$\frac{6}{5}$/iv iv   V$\frac{6}{3}$/vi vi   V$\frac{6}{5}$/VI VI   V$\frac{4}{4}$/V V⁶

V⁶/V V   V$\frac{4}{2}$/V V⁶   V⁶/iii iii   V²/VI VI⁶

Page 20

3. a. g minor

   b. VI$\frac{6}{4}$
   c. B♭
   d. V⁷/VI

   V⁷/VI   VI$\frac{6}{4}$

Page 20, cont.

4. a. a minor
   b. V^5_3
   c. B
   d. V^6_5/V

V^6_5/V V

5. a. A♭ Major
   b. IV^5_3
   c. A♭
   d. V^6_5/IV

V^6_5/IV IV

6. a. C♯ Major
   b. iii^6_3
   c. B♯
   d. V^6_4/iii

V^6_4/iii iii^6_3

7. a. F Major
   b. ii^5_3
   c. D
   d. V^7/ii

V^7/ii ii

Page 21, No. 8

a. Key of E♭ Major: V^7/ii ii^5_3;
   V/iii iii^5_3

Page 22

c. Key of C Major: V^6_5/V V^4_2

d. Key of E Major: V^7/V V^5_3;
   V^7/IV IV^5_3

LESSON 5: CADENCES, CHORD PROGRESSIONS, AUGMENTED SIXTH CHORDS (Pages 23-30)

Page 24

1.   I IV   V I
2. A Major
3.   IV V^7 I ii^6 I^6_4 V^7 I
4. Pivot chord
5. Authentic

6. A♭ Major

7.   I IV ii V   V/vi vi IV I
8. No
9. Secondary dominant
10. Plagal

Page 25

11. C Major
12. G Major
13. a. I^6_4
    b. V^5_3
    c. V^5_3
14. Half
15. c. I^5_3
    d. I^5_3
    e. IV^6_4
    f. V^6_5
16. Chord c

Page 26

17. G Major
18. D Major
19. I - $\underline{V}$
20. a. I$_3^5$
    b. $\underline{V}$$_5^6$
    c. $\underline{V}$^{7}/$\underline{IV}$
    d. $\underline{IV}$$_4^6$
    e. $\underline{V}$$_3^5$
21. e. I$_3^5$
    f. I$_3^5$
    g. $\underline{V}$$_3^4$
22. Secondary dominant
23. Pivot chord

Optional: Augmented 6th Chord

Page 28

24. It.$^{+6}$ $\underline{V}$ It.$_3^6$ $\underline{V}$ It.^{6} $\underline{V}$ IV$^{6\sharp}$ $\underline{V}$

25. Fr.$^{+6}$ $\underline{V}$ Fr.$_3^4$ $\underline{V}$ Fr.$_3^6$ $\underline{V}$ II$_{4\sharp}^6$ $\underline{V}$

26. Ger.$^{+6}$ $\underline{V}$ Ger.$_5^6$ $\underline{V}$ Ger.$_3^6$ I$_4^6$ II$_3^{6\sharp}$ I$_4^6$

27. (given)

Page 29

b. F Major: Ger.$^{+6}$ $\underline{V}$$_3^5$

c. D♭ Major: Fr.$^{+6}$ i$_4^6$

Page 30

d. d minor: It.$^{+6}$ $\underline{V}$$_3^5$

e. A♭ Major: Ger.$^{+6}$ I$_4^6$

f. A Major: Fr.$^{+6}$ I$_4^6$

REVIEW: LESSONS 1-5 (Pages 31-32)

Page 31, No. 1

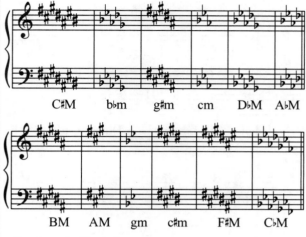

C♯M   b♭m   g♯m   cm   D♭M   A♭M

BM   AM   gm   c♯m   F♯M   C♭M

2. d melodic minor

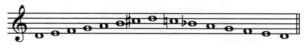

Lydian mode on B♭

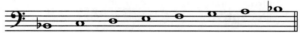

f harmonic minor

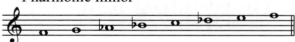

Whole tone on B

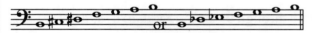

or

Chromatic on E

E♭ Major

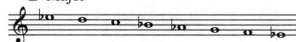

Page 32, No. 3

P5   m3   M7   A4   d8   M2   m6   d7

Page 32, cont. No. 4

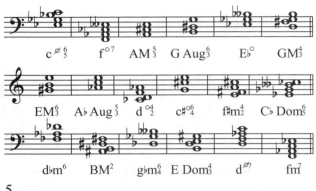

5.

6. V_3^6 ii_3^5 IV_3^6 V_3^4 iii_3^5 $vii°_3^5$

7. $ii°_4^6$ iv_3^5 $ii°_3^6$ VI_4^6 V_5^6 i_4^6

8. Authentic
    Plagal
    Half
    Deceptive

LESSON 6: TEXTURE AND COMPOSITIONAL TECHNIQUES (Pages 33-38)

Page 36

1 through 9: b, c, a, c, d, a, b, a, d

Page 37

10 through 12: a, c, d

13.

14. Theme
15. a. repetition
     b. sequence
     c. pedal point
     d. ostinato
16. No
17. Homophonic

Page 38

18. canon
19. polyphonic
20. contrapuntal

21.

LESSON 7: NONHARMONIC TONES AND MELODIC DEVICES

Page 42

1. a. passing tone
    b. suspension
    c. anticipation
    d. neighbor tone (upper neighbor)
    e. pivot chord
    f. neighbor tone (lower neighbor)

Page 43

    g. appoggiatura
    h. acciaccatura
    i. appoggiatura

2.

Page 44

3. a. anticipation
   b. neighbor tone (lower neighbor)
   c. neighbor tone (upper neighbor)
   d. passing tone

Page 45

   e. suspension
   f. acciaccatura
   g. appoggiatura

Page 46

4. Ger.$^{+6}$

5. Dominant
6. Harmony based on the interval of a third

LESSON 8: 20th & 21st CENTURY COMPOSITIONAL DEVICES (Pages 47-54)

Page 49

1. a. Twelve tone row
   b. Quartal harmony
   c. Atonality
   d. Bitonality (Polytonality)
   e. Polytonality

Page 50 (Enharmonics are acceptable)

(Any order acceptable)

Optional: Twelve Tone Analysis

Page 54
6. (Optional. Intervals have been simplified. enharmonics are acceptable)

Row →   ← Retrograde

	A2 down	m6 down	M2 up	m3 up	P5 down	A4 up	M2 up	P4 down	A4 up	M3 down	A4 up	
Series	C♯	B♭	D	E	G	C	F♯	A♭	E♭	A	F	B	Inversion ↓
A2 up	E	C♯	F	G	B♭	E♭	A	B	F♯	C	A♭	D	
m6 up	C	A	C♯	E♭	F♯	B	F	G	D	A♭	E	B♭	
M2 down	B♭	G	B	C♯	E	A	E♭	F	C	F♯	D	A♭	
m3 down	G	E	A♭	B♭	C♯	F♯	C	D	A	E♭	B	F	
P5 up	D	B	E♭	F	A♭	C♯	G	A	E	B♭	F♯	C	↑ Retrograde Inversion
A4 down	A♭	F	A	B	D	G	C♯	E♭	B♭	E	C	F♯	
M2 down	F♯	E♭	G	A	C	F	B	C♯	A♭	D	B♭	E	
P4 up	B	A♭	C	D	F	B♭	E	F♯	C♯	G	E♭	A	
A4 down	F	D	F♯	A♭	B	E	B♭	C	G	C♯	A	E♭	
M3 up	A	F♯	B♭	C	E♭	A♭	D	E	B	F	C♯	G	
A4 down	E♭	C	E	F♯	A	D	A♭	B♭	F	B	G	C♯	Retrograde Inversion

7. (Optional)

Series (Row)

Retrograde Inversion on D   Row on B

Inversion on C

Retrograde Inversion on E♭

Retrograde on A

REVIEW: LESSONS 6-8 (Pages 55-56)

Page 55

1. a. motive
   b. sequence
   c. canon
   d. ostinato
   e. augmentation
   f. repetition
   g. imitation
   h. diminution

Page 56

2. b, d, a, c

3.

4. anticipation, suspension, appoggiatura,
   neighbor tone (upper neighbor),
   passing tone, neighbor tone (lower neighbor)

5.

6.

7. a. polytonality
   b. atonality
   c. serialism
   d. twelve-tone row
   e. tertian harmony
   f. bitonality
   g. quartal harmony
   h. pivot chord

LESSON 4: THE FUGUE (Pages 57-66)

Assignment 1: Page 61.

1.

2. a. 2
   b. Tonal; subject begins with m2, answer
      begins with m3
   c. Dominant (5th); tonic is G; the tonal
      center of the answer is D

3. a. 5
   b. Tonic (I)

4. a. 6
   b. Dominant (5th)

5.

6. Meas. 12: B♭ Major, 3rd or relative
            Major

   Meas. 14: F Major, $\overline{V}$ / $\overline{III}$ ($\overline{V}$ of
            Relative Major)

   Meas. 16, beat 4: B♭ Major, 3rd or
            relative Major

   Meas. 20: c minor, iv or Subdominant

   Meas. 24: g minor, i or Tonic

Assignment 2: Page 62 (Optional)

1. a. (12)   h. 23
   b. 13   i. 28 (2nd half of beat 1)
   c. 15   j. 28 (2nd half of beat 3)
   d. 17 (2nd half of beat 1) k. 29
   e. 17 (2nd half of beat 3) l. 31
   f. 20   m. 33
   g. 21

2. a. Meas. 17 to 18
   b. Meas. 28 to 29

Page 62, cont.

3. a. 3   g. 17
   b. 5   h. 20
   c. 7   i. 22 (slightly modified)
   d. 12   j. 23 (slightly modified)
   e. 14   k. 28 (slightly modified)
   f. 15   l. 32

4. Meas. 1 to 7

5. a. Meas. 8 - 12   c. Meas. 24 - 27
   b. Meas. 18 - 20   d. Meas. 30 - 31

Page 63

6. Meas. 11-12: Key of B♭ Major
   V -I, Authentic

   Meas. 19-20: Key of c minor
   ii°^{6} - V, Half

   Meas. 24, beats 2-3: Key of g minor
   V -i, Authentic

   Meas. 27-28: Key of g minor
   iv^6 - V (E♭-G-C) or It^{+6} - V (E♭-G-C♯), Half

   Meas. 34: g minor
   V^7- I, Authentic

LESSON 10: SONATA FORM (Pages 67-82)

Assignment 1, Page 73

1. Exposition: Measure 1, page 74
   Development: Measure 57, page 77
   Recapitulation: Measure 83, page 79

2. Exposition:
   Theme 1: Meas. 1, page 74
   Bridge: Meas. 13, page 74
   Theme 2: Meas. 27, page 75

   Recapitulation:
   Theme 1: Meas. 83, page 79
   Bridge: Meas. 95, page 80
   Theme 2: Meas. 109, page 81

3. Exposition: F Major
   Theme 1: F Major
   Theme 2: C Major
   Development: C Major
   Recapitulation: F Major
   Theme 1: F Major
   Theme 2: F Major

4.   Exposition
   Theme 1   Theme 2
   F Major   C Major
   Tonic (I)   Dominant (V)

         Development
   Begins in   Ends in
   C Major   F Major
   Dominant (V)   Tonic (I)

         Recapitulation
   Theme 1   Theme 2
   F Major   F Major
   Tonic (I)   Tonic (I)

Assignment 2, Page 73 (Optional)

1. Harmonic analysis (Answers are listed
   below to match lines in the workbook)

Page 74

I   I   I   V^7/IV
IV$^6_4$ I
V$^6_5$ I   V$^4_3$ I^6 IV   V
V$^6_5$ I   vii°^{6} I^6 IV   V
I   V^7 I   V   I$^6_4$ V^7 I

Page 75

V   I$^6_4$ V^7 I   vi   I$^6_4$ b dim $^4_3$ V ^{6}
a dim $^4_3$ IV ^{6} I^6 g♯ dim $^4_3$ A Maj ^{6}
(cont) f♯ dim $^4_3$ G Maj ^{6} IV$^6_4$
e dim $^4_3$ I^6 ii^6
I$^6_4$ V   New key: C Major: I
V$^4_3$ I$^6_4$ V ^{6}

Page 76

V   V$^4_3$ I
V^7 I   I^6 ii^6
V$^6_5$/V   V   V$^6_5$/vi
vi   I$^6_4$ ii^6 I^6 ii^6 I$^6_4$ V^7
I   vii°^{6} I^6

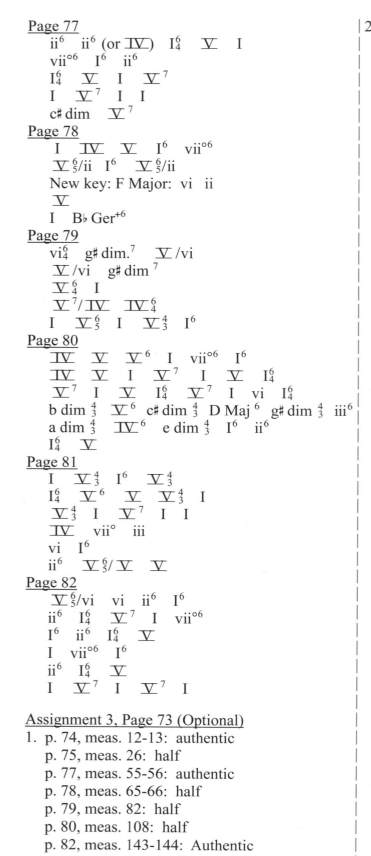

Page 77

ii⁶ ii⁶ (or IV) I⁶₄ V I

vii°⁶ I⁶ ii⁶

I⁶₄ V I V⁷

I V⁷ I I

c# dim V⁷

Page 78

I IV V I⁶ vii°⁶

V⁶₅/ii I⁶ V⁶₅/ii

New key: F Major: vi ii

V

I B♭ Ger⁺⁶

Page 79

vi⁶₄ g# dim.⁷ V/vi

V/vi g# dim⁷

V⁶₄ I

V⁷/IV IV⁶₄

I V⁶₅ I V⁴₃ I⁶

Page 80

IV V V⁶ I vii°⁶ I⁶

IV V I V⁷ I V I⁶₄

V⁷ I V I⁶₄ V⁷ I vi I⁶₄

b dim ⁴₃ V⁶ c# dim ⁴₃ D Maj ⁶ g# dim ⁴₃ iii⁶

a dim ⁴₃ IV⁶ e dim ⁴₃ I⁶ ii⁶

I⁶₄ V

Page 81

I V⁴₃ I⁶ V⁴₃

I⁶₄ V⁶ V V⁴₃ I

V⁴₃ I V⁷ I I

IV vii° iii

vi I⁶

ii⁶ V⁶₅/V V

Page 82

V⁶₅/vi vi ii⁶ I⁶

ii⁶ I⁶₄ V⁷ I vii°⁶

I⁶ ii⁶ I⁶₄ V

I vii°⁶ I⁶

ii⁶ I⁶₄ V

I V⁷ I V⁷ I

Assignment 3, Page 73 (Optional)

1. p. 74, meas. 12-13: authentic

p. 75, meas. 26: half

p. 77, meas. 55-56: authentic

p. 78, meas. 65-66: half

p. 79, meas. 82: half

p. 80, meas. 108: half

p. 82, meas. 143-144: Authentic

Level 10, Page 73

2. Sequence, page 74, meas. 5-6, and
page 79, meas. 87-88

Syncopation, page 74, measures 8 and 11

Sequence , page 75-76, meas. 28-34

Sequence, page 76, meas. 35-38

Sequence, page 76-77, meas. 43-46

Sequence, page 77, meas. 48-51

Pedal Point, page 78, meas. 63-66

Sequence, page 78, meas. 68-71

Imitation, page 81, meas. 117-120

Repetition and Pedal Point, page 79,
    meas. 78-79

Sequence, page 81, meas. 123-126

Sequence, page 79, meas. 80-81

Sequence, page 82, meas. 131-132 and
136-139

Syncopation, page 79-80, meas. 90 and 93

3. The Exposition and Recaptitulation are
    the same until measure 100. In measure
    100 (during the Bridge) the music changes
    to accomodate staying in tonic key.
    Measure 109 (Theme 2) is in the tonic
    key. The music is an exact transposition
    until measure 117, when sixteenths
    are used instead of triplets. Triplets
    then return in measure 123, which is
    a transposition of the Exposition until
    the end of the composition.

Sequence, page 81, meas. 110-115

4. Measure 6: Appoggiatura
    Measure 64: Appoggiatura

154

LESSON 11: RONDO FORM
(Pages 83-106)

Assignment 1, page 96

1a and 1b.

A: B♭ Major, I, page 97, upbeat to meas. 1
B: B♭ & F Majors, I & $\underline{V}$, page 98, meas. 18
A: B♭ Major, I, page 99, upbeat to meas. 44
C: g minor, vi (or relative minor), page 100, meas. 52
A: B♭ Major, I, page 101, upbeat to meas. 72
D: E♭ Major, $\underline{IV}$, page 102, meas. 90
A: B♭ Major, I, page 103, upbeat to meas. 115
B: B♭ Major, I, page 104, meas. 124 (This is the second theme of the B section; the first theme of the section of omitted)
A: B♭ Major, I, page 105, upbeat to meas. 143

Assignment 2, page 96

1. First repetition of A (measure 44): Only first half is repeated, exactly as beginning.

   Second repetition of A (measure 72): Exactly like beginning

   Third repetition of A (measure 115): Left hand has melody at beginning, then transfers to right hand. Only first half of A occurs.

   Fourth repetition of A (measure 143): Exactly as beginning, followed by coda

2. First time, B is in B♭ Major, then F Major
   Second time, B stays in B♭ Major

3. Measure 3: Appoggiatura
   Measure 12: Appoggiatura
   Measure 38: Suspension
   Measure 55: Appoggiatura
   Measure 59: Anticipation
   Measure 91: Upper Neighbor

4. It.+6

Assignment 3, page 97 (Optional)

1. Harmonic analysis. Answers are listed to match staff systems in the workbook.

Page 97
$\underline{V}$ ^{6}/ii   ii $\underline{V}$ ^{6} I   I^6
$\underline{IV}$ I^6 $\underline{V}$$^4_3$ I   I$^6_4$ $\underline{V}$ $\underline{V}$^{6}/ii   ii   ii^6 V$^6_5$
I   I^6 I^6 $\underline{IV}$ I$^6_4$ $\underline{V}$ I   I   ii   vii°
I   I^6 ii^6 vii°/$\underline{V}$ $\underline{V}$ I   ii   vii°   I $\underline{IV}$ $\underline{V}$ $\underline{V}$^{7}

Page 98
I $\underline{IV}$ $\underline{IV}$ I$^6_4$ $\underline{V}$^{7} I $\underline{IV}$
$\underline{IV}$ I$^6_4$ $\underline{V}$^{7} I $\underline{V}$^{7} I $\underline{V}$^{7} I
I $\underline{V}$^{6} in B♭ Major, I^6 in F Major
F Major (2 beats per chord): $\underline{V}$$^6_5$ I $\underline{V}$$^4_3$ I
$\underline{V}$$^6_5$ I $\underline{V}$$^4_3$ I^6 ii^6
I$^6_4$ $\underline{V}$^{7} I $\underline{V}$$^6_5$ $\underline{V}$$^4_3$ I^6

Page 99
I $\underline{V}$$^6_5$ $\underline{V}$$^4_3$ I   I^6
$\underline{IV}$ I^6 vi   ii^6 $\underline{V}$ I^6
$\underline{IV}$ $\underline{V}$
I $\underline{V}$^{7}/$\underline{IV}$ $\underline{IV}$$^6_4$ vii°^{6} I $\underline{V}$^{7}/$\underline{IV}$ $\underline{IV}$$^6_4$ vii°^{6}
I   vii°   I   vii°   I in F, $\underline{V}$ in B♭; B♭ M: $\underline{V}$^{6}/ii   ii $\underline{V}$^{6}
I   I^6 $\underline{IV}$ I^6 $\underline{V}$$^4_3$ I   I$^6_4$ $\underline{V}$ $\underline{V}$^{6}/ ii

Page 100
ii   ii^6 $\underline{V}$$^6_5$ I   I^6 I^6 $\underline{IV}$ $\underline{IV}$^{6} I$^6_4$ $\underline{V}$
I   g minor: i   ii° (or vii°$^4_3$ or f♯ dim $^4_3$)
vii°$^4_3$ i^6 $\underline{V}$^{6} i   ii°   i^6 $\underline{V}$^{6}/ iv
iv $\underline{VI}$ (or Ger^{+6})   i$^6_4$ $\underline{V}$
$\underline{V}$ vii°^{6} i   vii°$^4_4$ i^6
i$^6_4$ $\underline{V}$ i^6$\underline{V}$$^6_5$/iv   iv   vii°$^4_3$ (or f♯ dim $^4_3$)

Page 101
i$^6_4$ $\underline{V}$^{7} i   b dim $^4_3$ C Maj ^{6}
$\underline{V}$ B♭ Major: $\underline{V}$$^4_3$ $\underline{V}$^{6}/ii
ii $\underline{V}$^{6} I   I^6 $\underline{IV}$ I^6 $\underline{V}$$^4_3$ I
I$^6_4$ $\underline{V}$ $\underline{V}$^{6}/ ii   ii   ii^6 $\underline{V}$$^6_5$ I   I^6 I^6
$\underline{IV}$ $\underline{IV}$^{6} I$^6_4$ $\underline{V}$ I   ii   vii°   I   I^6 ii^6 vii°/ $\underline{V}$
$\underline{V}$ I   ii   vii°   I $\underline{IV}$ $\underline{V}$ $\underline{V}$^{7} I $\underline{IV}$

Page 102
$\underline{IV}$ I$^6_4$ $\underline{V}$^{7} I $\underline{IV}$ $\underline{IV}$ I$^6_4$ $\underline{V}$^{7}
I $\underline{V}$^{7} I $\underline{V}$^{7} I
E♭ Major: I $\underline{V}$$^6_5$ I
$\underline{V}$$^6_5$ I $\underline{IV}$
I   ii $\underline{V}$^{7} I^6 I
$\underline{IV}$ I   ii $\underline{V}$ I

Level 10, Pages 83-97

Page 103

vii°⁷/vi vi vii°⁷/$\overline{V}$

$\overline{V}^6$ $\overline{V}^6$ vi⁶ vii°⁶ I $\overline{V}^7$

I in E♭ $\overline{IV}$ in B♭ B♭ Maj: ii⁶ I$^6_4$ $\overline{V}$ $\overline{V}^4_3$/$\overline{V}$

$\overline{V}$ $\overline{V}^4_3$/$\overline{V}$ $\overline{V}$

I⁶ $\overline{V}^6_5$/ii ii $\overline{V}^6$ I

$\overline{V}^6_4$ $\overline{V}^6$ $\overline{V}^6_4$/$\overline{V}$ $\overline{V}$ $\overline{V}^4_2$/ii

Page 104

$\overline{V}^7$ $\overline{V}$ I$^6_4$ $\overline{V}$ $\overline{V}$ $\overline{V}^6$/$\overline{V}$

$\overline{V}$ I $\overline{V}^6_5$ $\overline{V}^4_3$ I⁶

I $\overline{V}^6_5$ $\overline{V}^4_2$ I⁶ I

$\overline{IV}$ I⁶ vi ii⁶ $\overline{V}$ I⁶

$\overline{IV}$ $\overline{IV}$

I⁶ ii⁶ $\overline{V}$ I $\overline{IV}^6_4$ vii°⁶

Page 105

I⁶ $\overline{V}^7$/$\overline{IV}$ $\overline{IV}$ vii°⁶ I⁶ $\overline{V}^6$

I vii°⁶ I⁶ $\overline{V}^6$/ii ii $\overline{V}^6$

I I⁶ $\overline{IV}$ I⁶ $\overline{V}^4_3$ I I$^6_4$ $\overline{V}$ $\overline{V}^6$/ii

ii ii⁶ $\overline{V}^6_5$ I I⁶ I⁶ $\overline{IV}$ $\overline{IV}^6$ I$^6_4$ $\overline{V}$

I I ii vii° I I⁶ ii⁶ vii°/$\overline{V}$ $\overline{V}$ I ii vii°

I $\overline{IV}$ $\overline{V}$ $\overline{V}^7$ I $\overline{IV}$ $\overline{IV}$ I$^6_4$ $\overline{V}^7$

Page 106

I $\overline{IV}$ $\overline{IV}$ I$^6_4$ $\overline{V}^7$ I $\overline{V}^7$ I $\overline{V}^7$

I $\overline{V}^7$ I $\overline{V}^7$ I

Assignment 4, page 97 (Optional)

1. p. 98, meas. 17-18: authentic
    p. 100, meas. 50-51: authentic
    p. 100, meas. 59: half
    p. 100, meas. 62-63: half
    p. 101, meas. 66-67: authentic
    p. 102, meas. 100-101: authentic
    p. 103, meas. 108-109: half
    p. 106, meas. 160-161: authentic

2. Sequence, page 97, meas. 1-2, page 99, meas. 43-45, page 101, meas. 71-73, page 103, meas. 114-116, page 105, meas. 142-144

Sequence, page 97, meas. 4-6, page 99-100, meas. 48-49, page 101, meas. 75-77, page 105, meas. 146-148

Repetition, page 98, meas. 12-16, page 101-102, meas. 83-87, page 105-106, meas. 154-158

Repetition, page 98, meas. 16-17, page 102, meas. 87-88, page 106, meas. 158-159

Repetition, page 98-99, meas. 28-31

Sequence, page 100, meas. 60-61

Sequence, page 100-101, meas.65-66

Repetition and Sequence, page 103,
    meas. 106-107

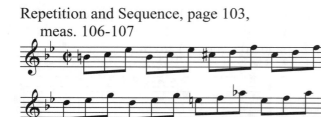

Repetition, page 106, meas. 159-161

LESSON 12: THEME AND VARIATIONS
    (Pages 107-122)

Page 115
1. F: I   vii°⁶ $\underline{V}_5^6$ I   ii⁶ $\underline{V}_2^4$ I⁶ $\underline{V}_5^6$ I $\underline{V}$

Page 116
$\underline{V}_3^4$ $\underline{V}_2^4$ I⁶ $\underline{IV}$ I⁶ $\underline{IV}$ I$_4^6$ $\underline{V}^7$ I
C: $\underline{V}_2^4$ I⁶   I $\underline{V}^6$ $\underline{V}$ I $\underline{V}_2^4$ I⁶   I $\underline{V}^6$ $\underline{V}$
I   F: $\underline{V}_2^4$ I⁶ $\underline{V}^6$ I $\underline{IV}$ I⁶ $\underline{IV}$ I$_4^6$ $\underline{V}^7$ I

2. Sixteenths, stepwise motion
No
No
3. Ties, suspensions
No
No
4. Chordal, many appoggiaturas,
    eighth note rhythm
No
No
5. Sixteenths with upbeats
No
Yes
6. Suspensions
Yes, to minor
No, but uses minor key
7. 32nd note rhythm
No
No
8. Dotted rhythms and 32nd notes
9. Measure 1: Appoggiatura
Measure 2: Appoggiatura
Measure 4: Appoggiatura
Measure 10: Appoggiatura
Measure 32-33: Suspension
Measure 33-34: Suspension
Measure 81: Suspension

LESSON 13: MUSIC HISTORY OVERVIEW AND TERMINOLOGY
(Pages 123-128)

Page 124, No. 1

a. 20th/21st Cent.
b. Baroque
c. Romantic
d. Classical
e. 20th/21st Cent.
f. Classical
g. Romantic
h. Romantic
i. Baroque
j. Classical
k. 20th/21st Cent.
l. 20th/21st Cent.
m. 20th/21st Cent.
n. Baroque
o. 20th/21st Cent.
p. Romantic
q. 20th/21st Cent.
r. Baroque
s. Romantic
t. Classical
u. 20th/21st Cent.
v. 20th/21st Cent.
w. Classical
x. Baroque
y. 20th/21st Cent.
z. Romantic

Page 128, No. 2

a. manner in which notes are executed, e.g. *staccato*
b. sharps, flats, naturals written before notes
c. shift of rhythm's pulse from 2 to 3
d. lightly
e. slight variation in rhythm
f. playfully
g. a sudden, sharp accent
h. dying away
i. half voice
j. contradiction of the meter: ♪ ♩ ♪
k. virtuosic piece with scales, rapid passages
l. without

REVIEW: LESSONS 9-13
(Pages 129-130)

Page 129

1. a. subject
   b. theme and variations
   c. exposition
   d. answer
   e. episode
   f. recapitulation
   g. theme 1 and theme 2
   h. real answer
   i. countersubject
   j. *stretto*
   k. development
   l. tonal answer
   m. rondo form

<u>Page 129</u>, No. 2. Allegro
                      Andante
                      Vivace

<u>Page 130</u>, No. 3 (Other composers and characteristics are possible)

Baroque composers:
- J.S. Bach
- Corelli
- Handel
- Rameau
- Scarlatti
- Telemann
- Vivaldi

Baroque characteristics:
- Polyphonic texture
- Use of ornamentation
- Improvisation
- Use of figured bass
- Dance Suite
- Keyboard instruments: Harpsichord, Clavichord, Organ
- Terraced Dynamics (*p mp mf f*)

Classical composers:
- Beethoven
- Clementi
- Czerny
- Diabelli
- Haydn
- Kuhlau
- Mozart

Classical characteristics:
- Homophonic texture
- Obvious cadence points
- Alberti bass
- Sonata form

Romantic composers:
- Brahms
- Chopin
- Dvořák
- Grieg
- Liszt
- Mendelssohn
- Schubert
- Schumann
- Tchaikovsky

Romantic characteristics:
- Programme music
- Descriptive titles
- Colorful harmonies and chromaticism
- Lyric melodies
- Complex rhythm patterns

Impressionism composers:
- Debussy
- Griffes
- Ravel

Impressionism characteristics:
- Unresolved dissonances
- Nonharmonic tones added to triads
- Parallel motion
- Whole-tone and pentatonic scales
- Irregular phrasing

20th/21st Century (Contemporary) composers:
- Bartók
- Britten
- Copland
- Dello Joio
- Kabalevsky
- Poulenc
- Prokofiev
- Shostakovich

20th/21st Century (Contemporary) characteristics:
- Less use of major and minor tonalities
- Quartal harmony
- Bitonality, Polytonality, Atonality
- Irregular and changing meters
- Polyphonic texture
- Neo-Classic writing
- Serial music
- Twelve-tone music

4. a. hold the note for its full value
   b. sustained
   c. immediately slower
   d. gradually slower
   e. chronological classification of a composer's music
   f. merrily, with humor

FINAL TEST (Pages 131-138)

<u>Page 131</u>, No. 1

Page 131, No. 2

f melodic minor

Mixolydian mode on C

c harmonic minor

whole tone on G

or

chromatic on D

C♭ Major

Page 132, No. 3

M2   P8   m6   d5   A8   d7   M3   P4

4.

e ⌀7   d m 6/4   e dim 6   F Aug 6/4   d♭°   f♯ d 4/2

D M 6/3   C♯ Aug 5/3   E♭ Dom 6/5   A♭ M 6   C M 6/4   b dim

G♭ Dom 7   b♭ m 6/4   F M 4/3   c♭ m 7   a °4/3   g ⌀7

5.

V 4/3/ V   V 6   V 7/ii   ii 6/4

V 4/2/iv   iv 6   V 6/5/ VI   VI

6. IV 6/3   vi 5/3   iii 6/4   V 6/3   ii 6/4   vii°5/3

7. V 4/3   ii°5/3   ii°6/3   iv 5/3   i 6/4   VI 6/4

8. Half, Authentic, Plagal, Deceptive

Page 133

9. a. Serialism
b. Pivot chord
c. Homophonic texture
d. Pedal point
e. Augmentation
f. Quartal harmony
g. Motive
h. Twelve-tone row
i. Tertian harmony
j. Ostinato
k. Theme
l. Polytonality
m. Polyphonic texture
n. Diminution
o. Atonality
p. Canon
q. Bitonality

Page 134

10.

11.

12. retrograde inversion

13. neighbor tone (upper neighbor)
passing tone
appoggiatura
anticipation

14. (Other composers and characteristics
are possible)

Baroque composers:

J.S. Bach	Scarlatti
Corelli	Telemann
Handel	Vivaldi
Rameau	

Page 134, cont.

Baroque characteristics:

    Polyphonic texture
    Use of ornamentation
    Improvisation
    Use of figured bass
    Dance Suite
    Keyboard instruments: Harpsichord,
        Clavichord, Organ
    Terraced Dynamics (*p mp mf f*)

Classical composers:

    Beethoven
    Clementi
    Czerny
    Diabelli
    Haydn
    Kuhlau
    Mozart

Classical characteristics:

    Homophonic texture
    Obvious cadence points
    Alberti bass
    Sonata form

Romantic composers:

    Brahms   Mendelssohn
    Chopin   Schubert
    Dvořák   Schumann
    Grieg   Tchaikovsky
    Liszt

Romantic characteristics:

    Programme music
    Descriptive titles
    Colorful harmonies and chromaticism
    Lyric melodies
    Complex rhythm patterns

Impressionism composers:

    Debussy
    Griffes
    Ravel

Impressionism characteristics:

    Unresolved dissonances
    Nonharmonic tones added to triads
    Parallel motion
    Whole-tone and pentatonic scales
    Irregular phrasing

20th/21st Century (Contemp.) composers:

    Bartók
    Britten
    Copland
    Dello Joio
    Kabalevsky
    Poulenc
    Prokofiev
    Shostakovich

20th/21st Century (Contemp.)characteristics:

    Less use of major and minor tonalities
    Quartal harmony
    Bitonality, Polytonality, Atonality
    Irregular and changing meters
    Polyphonic texture
    Neo-Classic writing
    Serial music
    Twelve-tone music

Page 135

15. E Major

16. a. IV_4^6

    b. V_3^5/vi

    c. vi_4^6

    d. I_4^6

    e. V_3^5

    f. vi_4^6

    g. iii_3^5

    h. IV_4^6

    i. I_3^5

Page 135, cont.

17. Plagal
18. syncopation
19. sequence
20. A♯ and C♮
21. Homophonic
22. Romantic

Page 137

23. F♯ Major
24. 3

25.

26. 3
27. Dominant (5th)
28. Tonal (Subject begins with 4th; answer begins with 5th)
29. 5
30. Tonic
31. Expositon
32. Episode
33. *stretto*
34. countersubject

Page 138

35. Walking tempo
36. D Major
37. A Major
38. a. D Major $\frac{5}{3}$
    b. A Dominant $\frac{6}{5}$
    c. a♯ diminished $\frac{6}{5}$
    d. b minor $\frac{6}{3}$
    e. A Major $\frac{6}{4}$
    f. E Dominant $\frac{6}{5}$
39. Chord e
40. Exposition
    Development
    Recapitulation
41. fast tempo